ALKALINE
pH 7—14

Alkaline Foods Cookbook
by Keith Exum

© 2007 Keith Exum

ISBN# 978-0-9768540-2-9
ISBN# 0-9768540-2-3

Utilizing Microsoft Publishing Software and Photoshop

Publisher: Jazzy Kitty Greetings Marketing & Publishing Co.
        406 Tartan Drive, Middletown, DE 19709

Scripture quotations are from the King James Version of the Holy Bible, New International Version and the New Living Translation.

Cover designed by: Keith Exum & Jazzy Kitty Greetings Marketing & Publishing Co.
Logo designed by: Keith Exum
Photography by: John Kollock of Philadelphia, PA
Associate Editor Molly Gandour

"If GOD DIDN'T MAKE IT, DON'T TAKE IT.

DON'T TAKE IT, IF GOD DIDN'T MAKE IT!"

Dr. SEBI

This book is dedicated to my children:

Rylund Keith Exum
&
Hunter Nubia Grayce Exum

With Love,

Your Father
Keith Exum

ACKNOWLEDGEMENTS

This book owes its existence to the countless researchers that influenced me throughout my years of study. The most influential of them is Dr. Sebi. I researched, and continue to explore his concepts; which compare the differences between alkaline foods versus acid and hybrid foods, and the healing properties of alkaline foods.

Dr. Sebi was litigated in the Supreme Court of New York in 1988. Witnesses came forth to testify that they had been cured by Dr. Sebi of many different types of pathologies, such as AIDS, Cancer, Diabetes, Leukemia, Sickle Cell Anemia, Impotency and blindness.

I am sincerely grateful to my mother Verla Mae Exum: my first teacher and supporter, who stood by me through thick and thin, with love, patience and care.

I would also like to thank Master Chef Michael Mosley for devoting his time and patience in helping me with a multitude of recipes and food preparation.

Many thanks to my editor Anelda Ballard, whose understanding and belief in my work played an important role in bringing this book to print. Also, thanks to the other editors/proofreader Molly Gandour, publicist, and staff at Jazzy Kitty Greetings Marketing & Publishing Company, whose professionalism and expertise assisted in the preparation and presentation of this book.

I wish to thank John "Rolex" Kollock for his outstanding photography.

Finally, to God all my family and friends, thank you for your love and encouragement and support.

Stay Alkaline!

Keith Exum

PREFACE

I was like most people when finding out about alkalinity, I wanted to know, what could I eat and how do I prepare and cook it? Being a Chef and herbalist for over 25 years, made it a lot easier for me than most to prepare, alter and come up with new cooking ideas. Some are under the impression that once you cook something that's alkaline you can destroy its alkalinity. This is far from the truth. For an example, tomatoes contain lycopene, a form of antioxidant. Raw tomatoes have a total antioxidant potential of about 80, but if you cook the tomatoes the antioxidant potential increases six-fold. This is because the raw tomato has been transformed to trans-lycopene in the cooked version do to the heat infusion, and trans-lycopene is much more readily absorbed by the body. This is the same with most foods.

Finally a book that gives you the alkaline food list, how to prepare and cook them, so you can remain healthy, energized, and vitalized.

Peace and Blessings,

Stay Alkaline!

Keith Exum, CEO
Alkaline Foods LLC

TABLE OF CONTENTS

TABLE OF CONTENTS

TABLE OF CONTENTS

TABLE OF CONTENTS

TABLE OF CONTENTS

Chapter 1

BECOMING ALKALINE

ALKALINITY 101

WHAT IS ALKALINE?

The word "alkali" comes from the Arabic "al-qalyan," meaning "base." This term was often used in pharmaceuticals by the Moors (Aboriginal Africans), who occupied the Iberian Peninsula around 711 A.D. You can visit the oldest pharmacy in Europe, which was established by the Moors, in the Penaranda de Duero, Spain.

Alkalinity measures the ability of a solution to neutralize acids. Alkalis are known to have pH (potential of hydrogen) greater than 7. Foods are classified as alkaline or acid, based on their oxidized remains and the amount and quality of their waste products. Alkaline foods produce very little waste and acidic foods produce large amounts of waste. The more acid, the more metabolic waste. But what does that mean for *you* and *your body*?

As Dr. A. Szent-Gyorgy stated, "The body is alkaline by design, but acidic by function." Every living cell within our body creates metabolized waste, which is acidic. As the nutrients from our food are delivered to each cell, the cells burn with oxygen in order to provide energy for us to live. The burned nutrients become metabolized waste. Whether you eat the best of foods or the worst, all foods generate metabolized waste. Most of our cells also go through metabolism, and these dead cells also become waste products.

All waste products are acid. Our body will discharge this waste through urine, bile, and perspiration. The problem is that our body can't get rid of 100% of the waste it produces, creating an over load of toxicity. Without proper elimination, these acid waste products become solid wastes, such as micro toxins, toxins, fungus, bacteria, and mucus. Unknown to us, they accumulate and build up in our blood, organs, and tissue. This accumulation of solid waste products accelerates the depletion of minerals and other nutrients, causes disease, and accelerates the aging process.

Our bodies work very hard to dispose of acidic waste, but eating acidic foods makes it harder and compounds the acid, making it even harder for our bodies to eliminate waste. Eating and drinking alkaline foods and water helps our bodies to remove and neutralize acidic waste products.

Meats, dairy products, sugar and starches are enemies of the human body. Meats produce uric acids, dairy produces lactic acids, and starches produce carbonic acids. As well, It is vitally important that we distinguish the difference between food and synthetics. 99% of corporate plant foods are either hybrids or genetically modified, therefore deeming them un-natural and acidic. These hybrids—white and brown rice, carrots, corn, potatoes, garlic, beans, soy, wheat, wheat grass, barley, and yams, to name a few—are high in starch and un-natural sugars, making them enemies of the body. Furthermore, any items that are inorganic, chemically sprayed, artificially sweetened, gassed, or dyed, or include additives, phosphoric acid, or caffeine are acidic and should be avoided. Read labels carefully, as almost everything in the grocery store falls into this category.

Just remember: all man made foods is un-natural and acidic. As Dr. Sebi states "if God didn't make it, don't take it!"

WHAT IS pH?

pH (potential of hydrogen) is a measurement of the acidity or alkalinity of a solution: the *lower* the pH the more *acidic* the solution, the *higher* the pH the more *alkaline (or base)*. The pH scale ranges from 0 to 14, with 0 thru 6.9 being acidic, 7 being neutral, and 7.1 through 14 alkaline. For example stomach juice has a pH of 1.5, wine 3.5, garlic 3.9, beer 4.4, acid rain 5, cow's milk 6.5, distilled water 7, blood 7.4, pancreatic juice 8.8, soap 9.1, and baking soda added to water 12.

All chemical processes have an ideal pH at which they are most efficient. For example the body functions best with an internal chemistry being alkaline (pH of 7.0 to 8.0). When this balance is compromised many problems can occur. Our cells die at pH 3.5. The pH of the blood is even more specific: if blood is at pH 7.4, it is normal. But if is just below, at pH 7.2—that equals death.

Our bodies produce lactic acid and carbon dioxide through movement. Since our bodies do not manufacture alkalinity, we must supply the alkalinity from an outside source to keep our bodies alkaline. Ideally there is adequate amount of alkalinity in the diet to do this. However, if there is not, the body must extract alkaline from its organs, tissue, and bones to neutralize the acid. This causes the body to become acidic, and thus diseased.

FASTING

Fasting for religious and spiritual reasons has been a part of the human culture since pre-history. It is mentioned in many holy texts, such as the Kemetic (Egyptian) texts, Mahabharata, Upanishads, Olmec texts (pre-Columbus), the Torah, Bible and the Qur'an. For a perfect example, see the Book of Daniel in the Old Testament of the Bible, from verses 1 through 20.

Fasting is willingly abstaining from some or all foods and/or drinks for a period of time. Depending on the tradition, fasting practices may forbid consumptions of certain types of food. Fasting is a highly recommended, though optional, step towards achieving alkalinity.

If you have never started a fast before, try fasting for half a day, for 7 days. Don't eat any thing in the morning, from the time that you awake until 4 p.m. Then, don't eat past 8 p.m. and drink plenty of water, at least one gallon throughout the day. Try adding Alkaline Foods Green Food plus Mix for added chlorophyll and nutrients (pg 131).

Depending on the type of fast you chose weather it is for religious and spiritual reasons or detoxification, weather you sustain from eating anything or from just eating acidic foods. These recipes can be a good form of fasting. For detoxification and over acidity it is recommended to try fasting without eating anything for seven (7) days, just 3 liters or one (1) gallon of alkaline water that has a pH above 8.5 throughout the day.

Then try fasting for 24 hours. Once you have a feel for what fasting does for you, you can elevate to a 7 day fast, then to a 21 day fast, which is the best. If at any time during your fast you feel that you can't take it any longer, try eating some sea moss porridge or drinking some almond milk mixed with sea moss. (pg. 26). The sea moss will make you feel as if you had something to eat.

You may be afraid that your strength will diminish due to the catabolism of muscular protein fibers, but this fear is unwarranted. Starvation will occur only when the body is forced to use vital tissue to survive. Although protein is being used by the body during the fast, a person fasting even for 40 days on water will not suffer a deficiency of protein, vitamins, minerals or fatty acids. In the breakdown of unhealthy cells, all essential substances are used and conserved in a most extraordinary manner. Even during long fasts, the number of muscle fibers remains the same. Although the healthy cells may be reduced in size and strength for a time, they remain perfectly sound.

Fasting triggers a truly wondrous cleansing process that reaches right down to each and every cell and tissue in the human body. Since you are not putting these acidic foods into your body, the body then can cleanse itself and neutralize the acids more rapidly by fasting. It is the safest and fastest way to unmask bad health and detoxify the human body. Before trying or changing any diet program always consult with your health provider.

WELCOME TO A NEW WAY OF LIFE AND LONGEVITY!
The diet recommended in this cookbook will provide your body with the proper environment for the best nutrition and the best health. All foods that we recommend are alkaline. These foods are electrifying and energizing and should be eaten on a daily basis. If your favorite foods are not listed, you should abstain from eating them.

Stay Alkaline!

ALKALINE FOODS LIST

Below are foods that belong in your kitchen and in your diet, to make you feel great. These foods are perfect ingredients for the recipes in this book, and for you to experiment with on your own! The majority of these items can probably be found in your local supermarket. Others may require a bit more detective work. Try Latin, Asian, and Caribbean grocery stores, health food stores, or farmers' markets. Remember to buy organic and local, whenever possible.

Note on some omitted foods: Refined sugar and foods high in oxalic acid (spinach, cranberries, garlic and rhubarb) leach calcium and iron from the body. Though fresh, raw spinach and asparagus are rich in vitamins, they contain oxalic acid, a substance which interferes with the absorption and assimilation of iron & calcium by the digestive system. Garlic is undesirable because it contains mustard oil – an ingredient that disrupts the action of certain digestive enzymes.

FRUITS
Acai
Apricots
Avocadoes
Black Currants
Bananas (small/medium, *use sparingly*)
Berries (all varieties EXCEPT cranberries)
Camu Camu (also known as Cacari or Camo Camo)
Citron
Dates
Elderberries
Figs
Grapes (with seeds)
Guavas
Guinepps
Jelly Coconuts (young, green coconuts with a soft, jelly-like interior)
Limes (key limes preferred, with seeds)
Lychee
Mangoes
Melons (with seeds: try cantaloupes, honeydew, watermelon, etc.)
Oranges (Seville or sour preferred)
Papayas
Passion Fruit

FRUITS *(Continued)*
Pears
Peaches
Plums
Pomegranate
Pomelo
Prunes
Raisins
Sacha Inchi (powerful omega-3)
Sea Buckthorn
Soursops
Sugar Apples (cherimoya)

VEGETABLES
Amaranth Greens (also known as Callaloo, Chinese spinach or Hinn Choy)
Anamu Leaves
Bell Peppers
Broccoli (raw or steamed, *use sparingly*)
Cabbage (green)
Cactus Pads and Flowers (Nopales or Izote)
Chayote
Chives
Cucumbers
Dandelion Greens
Ginger
Jicama
Kale
Leeks
Lettuce (all *EXCEPT* iceberg—experiment with romaine, arugula, etc.)
Mushrooms *(except shitake)*
Mustard Greens
Okra *(use sparingly)*
Olives
Onions (red preferred)
Plantain (ripe)
Pumpkin or Calabaza
Sarsaparilla
Scallions
Squash
Tomatoes (*ONLY* cherry or plum)
Tomatillo

VEGETABLES *(Continued)*
Turnip Greens *(not the root)*
Zucchini

SEA VEGETABLES
Agar Agar
Bladder Wrack
Hijiki
Iceland Moss
Kelp
Nori or Sushi Wrap (toasted or untoasted)
Sea Moss or Irish Moss
Wakame

OIL
Extra Virgin Olive Oil

GRAINS
Amaranth
Black Rice
Quinoa
Rye
Spelt
Teff
Wild Rice

NUTS
Almonds
Sesame Seeds (or Tahini Butter)
Walnuts

DRINKS AND MILKS
Almond Milk
Coconut Milk (from Jelly Coconuts)
Root Beer (natural)
Sarsaparilla
Sea Moss Drink

SEASONINGS & SPICES
* Salty:

SEASONINGS & SPICES *(Continued)*
Dulse
Herbamare
Kelp
Sage
Sea Salt
Tarragon
Thyme
Trocomare
Vegesal
* Mild:
Basil
Bay Leaf
Coriander
Dill
Parsley
Nutmeg
Onion Powder
* Spicy:
Cayenne
Chili Powder
Cinnamon
Cumin
* Savory:
Tumeric

NATURAL SWEETENERS
Agave Nectar or Syrup
Maple Syrup (grade B or C)
Nopales, Prickly Pear Nectar or Syrup

ORGANIC OR WILD CRAFT TEAS
Anise
Black Chohsh
Bladder Wrack
Blueberries
Blueberry Leaf
Burdock Root
Cinnamon
Dandelion (roasted roots)
Elderberries

ORGANIC OR WILD CRAFT TEAS *(Continued)*

Fennel
Fenugreek
Ginger
Green Tea
Lemon Grass
Milk Thistle (may promote liver functioning)
Corn Silk
Red Clover
Red Raspberries
Rooibos Tea (South African caffeine-free red tea)
Sarsaparilla
Sea Moss
White Tea
Wu Long
Yellow Dock

WATER

Distilled Water (*ONLY* for cooking)
Purified (for drinking with a pH above 8.5)
Spring Water (for drinking with a pH above 8.5)
Young Coconut Water (fresh, *NOT* packaged)

MISCELLANEOUS

Achiote: natural red food coloring
Cutty: natural yellow food coloring
Natural Tomato Paste
Natural Tomato Sauce
Natural Almond Extract
Natural Vanilla Extract

KITCHEN EQUIPMENT

* STAINLESS STEEL POTS AND PANS

* STAINLESS STEEL *OR* WOOD UTENSILS

* HIGH SPEED BLENDER: I recommend a Cuisinart model. Check your local kitchen store, or www.cuisinart.com.

* HIGH SPEED ELECTRIC JUICER: Manual juicers are good for travel and for small amount of fruit juice, but are very time consuming. The Champion Juicer is my recommended model. Because it operates on the mastication process, the Champion Juicer preserves more fiber, enzymes, vitamins and trace minerals.   It produces dark, sweet juice with rich, full-bodied flavor. The Champion Juicer can be found at many health food and specialty kitchen stores. Check online at www.championjuicer.com to find a store in your area.

* FOOD PROCESSOR: Again, I recommend a Cuisinart model. Check your local kitchen store, or www.cuisinart.com.

Chapter 2

SOME OF THE BEST FOODS ON EARTH

PART ONE: GRAINS

"And God said, 'Behold, I have given you every herb bearing seed, which is upon the face of all the earth, and every tree, in the which is the fruit of a tree yielding seed; to you it shall be for meat. And to every beast of the earth, and to every fowl of the air, and to every thing that creepeth upon the earth, wherein there is life, I have given every green herb for meat:' and it was so." (Gen. 1:29-30, KJV)

Grains have been a nutritional staple for civilizations since the dawn of time. However, today it can be extremely difficult to find grains that are not in some way synthetic, hybrids, or genetically modified—all of which produce acidity in our bodies. The grains below have millennia's-old genetic make-ups that will both please your palate and nurture your body.

AMARANTH

Amaranth has been touted as a miracle grain, a super grain, and the grain of the future. A dietary staple of the Aztec empire, this ancient crop was "lost" for hundreds of years, and only since the Sixties, following its rediscovery, has it been grown in the U.S.

The leaves of the amaranth plant taste much like spinach and are used in the same manner that spinach is used. They are best if consumed when the plant is young and tender. Amaranth seed is high in protein (15-18%) and contains respectable amounts of lysine and methionine, two essential amino acids not frequently found in grains. It is high in fiber and contains calcium, iron, potassium, phosphorus, and vitamins A and C. The fiber content of amaranth is three times that of wheat and its iron content, five times more than wheat. It contains two times more calcium than milk.

Using amaranth in combination with quinoa and spelt results in a complete protein as high in food value as fish, red meat or poultry. Amaranth also contains tocotrienols (a form of vitamin E), which have cholesterol lowering activity. Cooked amaranth is 90% digestible and because of this ease of digestion, it has traditionally been given to those recovering from an illness or ending a fasting period. Amaranth consists of 6-10% oil, which is found mostly within the germ. The oil is predominantly unsaturated and is high in linolic acid.

BLACK RICE (LONG GRAIN)
Real wild rice grows is not genetically modified, like most of the other grains available in the US. While the hybrids all have less nutrients that their ancestors, real wild rice is as nutritious and powerful as ancient grains.

Most "wild" rice available in grocery stores across the country is actually cultivated in rice paddies. It cooks uniformly, is consistent year after year, and is actually a hybrid developed by the University of Minnesota. It is because of this rice that many people do not like wild rice. Believe me: there is a great deal of difference between real wild rice and this paddy rice! To me there is no comparison.

Real wild rice requires just the right conditions to grow and only grows naturally in northern Minnesota and Canada. The water has to be at a certain level, and it needs to flow slightly, but not so much as to uproot the plants. These non-depleted soils at the bottom of pristine lakes give the black rice rich flavor and nutrition.

QUINOA (pronounced keen-wa)
Quinoa has been a staple food of millions for almost 5,000 years, and is know with great respect as the "Mother Grain." It comes from the Andes Mountains of South America, and was one of the three staple foods of the Inca civilization.

Quinoa contains more protein than any other grain: an average of 16.2 percent. Some varieties of quinoa are more than 20 percent protein. Furthermore, this protein is of an unusually high quality. It is high in lysine, methionine, and cystine, and is a complete protein. Lastly, quinoa is a 35 on the glycemic index, making it a good wheat or gluten replacement for those with allergies or diabetic needs.

SPELT
Spelt was introduced to the United States in the 1890s. In the 20th century, spelt was virtually replaced by wheat, which produces higher yields. However, since spelt is rather hardier than wheat and does not require fertilizers, the organic farming movement made it more popular again towards the end of the century.

Spelt contains about 62 percent carbohydrate, 8.8 percent fiber, 12 percent protein and 2.7 percent fat, as well as dietary minerals and vitamins, including silica. As it contains a high amount of gluten, spelt is suitable for

SPELT *(Continued)*

baking. Its gluten is different from that in wheat and, therefore, spelt can sometimes be consumed by those with gluten allergies.

TEFF

The use of Teff can be traced back to about 3359 BC. It was produced and used primarily around Ethiopia, India, and Australia. While Teff still provides over two-thirds of the human nutrition in Ethiopia, it is still relatively unknown elsewhere. Recently, some private entrepreneurs in the U.S. have begun cultivating Teff.

Teff is the smallest grain in the world: it takes 150 teff grains to weigh as much as one wheat grain! Teff may be substituted for seeds, nuts or other small grains when baking, as a thickener for soups, stews, gravies and puddings, to make grain burgers, or in stir fries and casseroles.

Nutritionally Teff consists mainly of bran and germ, and contains no gluten, a source of many food allergies. Teff is rich in calcium, phosphorous, iron, copper, aluminum, barium and thiamin, and is a good source of protein, amino acids (especially lysine), carbohydrates and fiber.

PART TWO: SEA VEGETABLES

"And by the river upon the bank thereof, on this side and on that side, shall grow all trees for meat, whose leaf shall not fade, neither shall the fruit thereof be consumed: it shall bring forth new fruit according to his months, because their waters they issued out of the sanctuary: and the fruit thereof shall be for meat, and the leaf thereof for medicine." (Ezekiel 47:12)

Sea vegetables are also known as seaweeds, algae or marine algae. Most of us unknowingly eat processed sea vegetables every day. Manufacturers use them as thickeners and stabilizers in such products as ice cream, instant pudding, whipped toppings, salad dressings, and even toothpaste. But unprocessed sea vegetables haven't caught on much outside of Asia——which is a shame, because they're packed with vitamins, minerals and protein, yet low in calories.

Sea vegetables contain more minerals than any other foods. A wide range of minerals account for up to 38 percent of their dry weight. According to Seibin and Teruko Arasaki, authors of *Vegetables from the Sea*, "All of the minerals required by human beings, including calcium, sodium, magnesium, potassium, iodine, iron, and zinc are present in sufficient amounts. In addition, there are many trace elements in seaweeds." Sea vegetables also contain important vitamins, including vitamin A (in the form of beta-carotene), B1, B2, B6, niacin, vitamin C, pantothenic acid, and folic acid. There are even trace amounts of vitamin B12, which rarely occurs in land vegetables.

Besides their impressive nutritional profile, high quality sea vegetables offer other important health benefits. For centuries, Oriental medicine has recognized that sea vegetables contribute to general well being, especially for the endocrine and nervous systems. In recent decades, medical researchers have discovered that a diet including sea vegetables reduces the risk of some diseases.

Sea vegetables classified as *brown algae*—including arame, hijiki, kombu and wakame—have been shown to cleanse the body of toxic and acidic pollutants. Specifically, scientific research has demonstrated that these plants, which are abundant in alginic acid, bind with any heavy metals in the intestines, render them indigestible, and cause them to be eliminated from the body.

You can usually find plastic bags of dehydrated sea vegetables in health food stores, or in the Asian foods section of larger supermarkets. After re-hydrating, chop them up and add them to salads, soups, stews, or stir fries.

ARAME

This popular seaweed is very sweet and mild, and it's loaded with iron, calcium, and iodine. It's virtually fat-free, low in calories, and rich in protein and trace minerals.

BLADDERWRACK (*Fucus vesiculosus*)

Bladderwrack is also known by the names Black Tang, Rockweed, Bladder Fucus, Seawrack, Sea Oak, Black Tany, Cut Weed, and Rockwrack. Discovered in 1812, this seaweed was the original source of medical iodine, and was used extensively to treat goiter, a swelling of the thyroid gland related to insufficient iodine. In the 1860s, it was claimed that Bladderwrack, as a thyroid stimulant, could counter obesity by increasing metabolic rate, and, since then, it has been featured in numerous weight-loss remedies.

Where obesity is associated with thyroid trouble, this herb may be very helpful in reducing the excess weight. It has a reputation in helping the relief of rheumatism and rheumatoid arthritis, both used internally and as an external application upon inflamed joints. A chemical constituent of Bladderwrack called alginic acid swells upon contact with water; when taken orally, it forms a type of "seal" at the top of the stomach, and for this reason is used in several over-the-counter preparations for heartburn. The same constituent gives Bladderwrack laxative properties as well. Other proposed uses of Bladderwrack include treating athero-sclerosis and strengthening immunity, although there is no scientific evidence at present that it works for these purposes.

Bladderwrack is found on the coasts of the North Sea, the western Baltic Sea, and the Atlantic and Pacific Oceans. It is commonly found as a component of kelp tablets or powders used as nutritional supplements. It is sometimes loosely called "kelp," but that term technically refers to a different seaweed. Primary chemical constituents of this plant include mucilage, algin, mannitol, beta-carotene, zeaxanthin, iodine, bromine, potassium, volatile oils, and many other minerals.

DULSE (*Palmaria palmate*)

Dulse, known in Nova Scotia as Sea Parsley, is nutrient dense, red seaweed that grows in the North Atlantic and the Pacific Northwest. The seaweed grows attached to rocks in the inter-tidal zone, where the water is cold, the current is swift, and the ocean bottom is clean. Dulse grows so quickly in the summer that it can be picked every two weeks.

Dulse is eaten as a tasty snack in Nova Scotia. It can be eaten sun-dried, fried, baked with cheese, or fresh off the rocks. Dulse can also be used as a condiment or sprinkled on salads and soups. It's salty, so it makes a great salt substitute. It is a great nutritional supplement due to its high concentrations of Vitamin B6 and B12, iron, fluoride, potassium, and protein.

GLASSWORT

Glasswort is also known as Hair Vegetable, Black Moss, Hair Sea-weed, and Fat Choy. It is used in Chinese soups, and as a garnish. It can be found in Chinese markets and pharmacies.

HIJIKI or HIZIKI

Hijiki has a mild flavor, so it's a good choice if you want to slip a sea vegetable unobtrusively into your soups and stews in order to fortify them with calcium, iron, and other nutrients. When re-hydrated, it roughly quadruples in size, so a little goes a long way. If you can't find hijiki, you can substitute arame (doesn't expand as much when re-hydrated), or dulse.

IRISH MOSS or SEA MOSS (*Chondrus crispus*)

Irish Moss is also known by the names Pearl Moss and Carrageenan. This plant is found on the Atlantic coast of both Europe and North America. Irish Moss was used medicinally by the Irish during the famine of the 19th century. It has also been used as a mattress stuffing, as cattle feed, and as ink thickener.

The primary role of this herb was as a medicine, in speeding recuperation from debilitating illness, especially tuberculosis & pneumonia. Herbs such as Irish Moss and other tonic nutritive remedies have much to offer in facilitating proper recovery of health. It was used to treat respiratory illnesses, as well as digestive conditions where a demulcent is called for, such as gastritis, ulceration of the stomach, and duodenum. It has been used to treat inflammations of the urinary system. It has also been used in maintenance diets for diabetes patients. Recent animal research has shown

Irish Moss to exhibit an anti-viral property against influenza B and the mumps viruses. Studies have also confirmed the herb's value in treating ulcers, and to use it as an anti-coagulant.

The primary chemical constituents of Irish Moss include protein, polysaccharides, iodine, bromine, mucilage, carrageens, beta carotene, and vitamin B-1. The mucilage present in Irish Moss is used in large quantities by the food industry to make jellies and as a smooth binder, adding texture and stability to ice cream, whipped cream, puddings, soups, and salad dressings. It has also been used as a thickening agent in cosmetics, and used in lotions to soften skin and to prevent premature wrinkling.

KOMBU or KONBU
Kombu is also known as Tangle, Sea Tangle, Oarweed, Sea Cabbage, and Kelp. It's very popular in Japan, where it's used to flavor dashi, a soup stock. Konbu is usually sold dried, in strips or sheets. Choose konbu that's very dark, almost black, and don't wipe off the white residue that often appears on the surface; it's very flavorful.

LAVER (pronounced LAY-ver)
Laver is also called Purple Laver, Purple Seaweed, Nori, and Redware. The name nori is also used for laver because sushi nori is made from laver. However, unlike sushi nori, laver should be re-hydrated before use.
This protein-rich seaweed is popular in Britain and Japan. To re-hydrate, soak it in water for about an hour, then add it to soups and salads. If you can't find laver, you can substitute sushi nori.

NAMA WAKAME
Nama wakame is Japanese for "raw seaweed." Look for bags of this heavily salted seaweed in Japanese or Korean markets.

NORI or SUSHI NORI
Nori is also called Laver, Marsh Samphire, or Seaweed Sheets. These thin dark sheets are used to make sushi. They're usually a dark purplish black, but they turn green and acquire a pleasant, nutty flavor when toasted. "Yaki" means "cooked" in Japanese, so pretoasted nori sheets are labeled "yaki-nori" or "yaki sushi nori." You can also make your own toasted nori sheets by passing nori sheets over a flame a few times. Look for toasted and untoasted sushi nori in the Asian foods section of large supermarkets. If you can't find nori, a possible substitution is soybean paper.

PASSE-PIERRE

Passe-pierre is also called Pousse-pierre, Purple Laver, Purple Seaweed, Rock Samphire, Sea Green Bean, Salicornia, Marsh Samphire, Sea Pickle, and Glasswort. The crisp, salty sprigs make terrific garnishes. It's sometimes available fresh in the summer. If not, look for a pickled version in specialty food shops. It's more commonly found in Europe than in the U.S.

WAKAME (pronounced wah-KAH-may)

Wakame is also called Alaria. It has a sweet flavor, and it's rich in calcium. It's often rehydrated and then added to soups or sautéed as a side dish. Dry wakame can also be toasted and crumbled over salads and other dishes. If you can't find it, you may substitute sea lettuce, dulse, or arame.

PART THREE: MUSHROOMS

"Let your food be your medicine, and your medicine be your food." Hippocrates (430 - 370 B.C.)

Based on hieroglyphics dating back 4600 years, the Egyptians believed that eating mushrooms could make them immortal, but they prohibited anyone outside of the royal family from eating mushrooms. The Romans believed mushrooms were the foods for the gods. Hippocrates prescribed mushrooms for healing, while Eastern and other cultures have used mushrooms to treat colds and flu, indigestion, high blood pressure, high cholesterol, and infection. Mushrooms are said to have anti-viral, anti-cancer, and aphrodisiacal qualities because of its source of a trace mineral called Germanium. Germanium serves as an electrical semiconductor, helping correct distortions in the electrical fields of the body. Cultures around the world believed that they could make people super strong and elevate the soul.

CRIMINI

Criminis are a brown variety of the common white mushroom, and may be referred to as Italian brown mushrooms. They have a much more intense and earthy flavor than the white variety. Their texture is also firmer then the white.

ENOKI

Enokis appear almost flower-like, as they grow upright in bunches. They have a mild, light flavor and are slightly crunchy. They can be used in salads.

OYSTER

Oyster mushrooms vary by species coming in many different colors, ranging from white or gray, to pink or yellow. They can rage in size from 1 to 3 inches.

PORTABELLA

The portabella is actually an overgrown Crimini mushroom. The longer growing cycle, along with the characteristic opened cap give this mushroom an exquisite, meaty flavor and taste.

WHITE (*Agricus bisporus*)

White mushrooms vary in color from white to light brown. They can range in size from small to large. Use raw for salads and vegetable trays. Marinated, stuffed, or sautéed, they are the perfect vegetable to compliment any meal.

Chapter Three

BREAKFAST

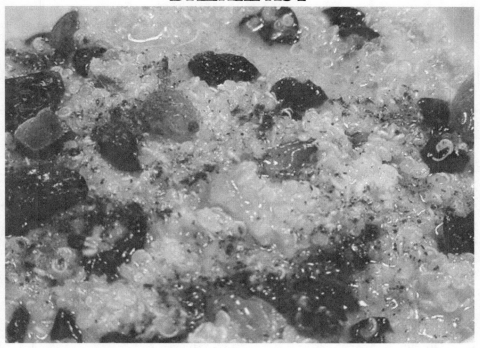

(Hot Quinoa Breakfast with Dried Fruit (pg 27)

Morning Power Smoothie

2 servings (8 oz glasses)
Prep and Cook Time: 5 minutes

This smoothie gives you a delicious way to enjoy the nutritional benefits of strawberries. The added tahini will help to sustain you for a healthy fruit pick-me-up.

Ingredients

- 4 large strawberries
- 1 cup fresh orange juice
- 1 Tbsp tahini
- 1 medium size banana
- ½ tsp vanilla
- 1 Tbsp agave nectar
- 8 oz glass of spring or alkaline water
- ½ lime, squeezed into the water

Preparation

1. Remove stems from strawberries and wash.
2. Blend all ingredients in blender until smooth.

Almond Milk

4 servings (8 oz glasses)
Prep and Cook Time: 10 minutes

> VARIATION: Blend in 1 tsp Irish Moss powder, a pinch of nutmeg and cinnamon, and some of your favorite berries from our Alkaline Foods List to make a high nutrition and very tasty beverage.

Ingredients

- 1 cup soaked almonds (soak in a bowl in the refrigerator overnight and rinse before using)
- 1 liter distilled or spring water
- 1 Tbsp sea moss powder or freshly cooked sea moss
- 1 vanilla bean, seeds scooped out
- ½ cup maple syrup or agave nectar

Preparation

1. Blend the soaked almonds with the water until smooth.
2. Then strain the mixture through a cheesecloth or strainer into a big bowl. Save the almond pulp in a container and put in the refrigerator for later use.
3. Put the almond milk back into the blender and blend in the vanilla seeds and some of the maple syrup and/or agave nectar, until smooth. Add sweetener as you wish; sweeten to taste.
4. This milk will last in the refrigerator for about 3-5 days. Shake well before using.

Irish Moss Beverage

6-8 servings (8 oz glasses)
Prep and Cook Time: 20 minutes

Also makes a delicious and healthy dessert!

Ingredients

- ➤ 2 oz Irish Moss (if you have powdered sea moss use 1 Tbsp)
- ➤ 6-8 cups water
- ➤ 1 cup sweetened almond milk (optional)
- ➤ maple syrup or agave nectar (sweeten to taste)
- ➤ ½ ground or grated nutmeg
- ➤ 1 Tbsp vanilla

Preparation

1. Wash Irish Moss thoroughly to remove sand before boiling.
2. Over high heat, combine moss, water, and boil uncovered for about 30 minutes.
3. Remove from stove to cool.
4. Add an extra cup of water if moss is too thick.
5. Strain liquid.
6. Discard remaining moss mixture.
7. Set aside to cool mixture.
8. Blend mixture with remaining ingredients: vanilla, almond milk, nutmeg and maple syrup or agave nectar.
9. Refrigerate and serve cool.

Hot Quinoa Breakfast with Dried Fruit

4 servings
Prep and Cook Time: 30 minutes

This healthy hot breakfast is so good, you may feel like you are eating dessert.

Ingredients

- 2½ cups fresh orange juice
- 1 Tbsp fresh lime juice
- 1 tsp finely minced lime zest
- ¼ cup maple syrup
- ¾ cup coarsely chopped walnuts
- 15 pitted prunes
- 10 dried apricots, cut in half
- ¼ tsp cinnamon
- 1 cup quinoa
- 4 cups lightly salted water (use sea salt)

Preparation

1. Combine the orange juice, lime juice, zest, cinnamon and maple syrup in a medium sized saucepan and stir.
2. Bring to a simmer on high heat, and add prunes and apricots.
3. Turn the heat to the lowest level. Simmer gently for about 10 minutes. Don't let the prunes get too soggy. While prunes are simmering, start cooking quinoa by bringing lightly salted water to a boil in a medium saucepan.
4. Add quinoa to boiling water, stirring slowly and constantly.
5. Reduce heat to low and cook for about 15 minutes, stirring to make sure it doesn't get lumpy. If it starts to get too thick, add a little more hot water. You want it to be soft.
6. Remove fruit from sauce to a shallow bowl, using a slotted spoon. Turn the heat to high.
7. Reduce the liquid to about half, return fruit and add walnuts to sauce, and serve over bowl of quinoa.

Amaranth "Grits"

2 servings
Prep and Cook Time: 25 minutes

Ingredients

➤ 1 cup amaranth
➤ 1 medium onion, finely chopped
➤ 3 cups water or vegetable stock (broth) (pg 95)
➤ sea salt
➤ hot sauce to taste
➤ garnish: 2 cherry tomatoes

Preparation

1. Combine the amaranth, onion, and stock in a 2-quart saucepan. Boil; reduce heat and simmer covered until most of the liquid has been absorbed, about 20 minutes.
2. Stir well. If the mixture is too thin or the amaranth not quite tender. It should be crunchy, but not gritty hard.
3. Boil gently while stirring constantly until thickened, about 30 seconds.
4. Add sea salt to taste.
5. Stir in a few drops of hot sauce, if desired, and garnish with chopped tomatoes.

Quinoa Muffins

12 servings
Prep and Cook Time: 40 minutes

Ingredients

- ➢ 1 cup quinoa flour
- ➢ 1 tsp non-aluminum baking powder
- ➢ ½ tsp baking soda
- ➢ 1/4 tsp sea salt
- ➢ 1/3 cup almond butter
- ➢ 1 tsp natural vanilla extract
- ➢ 1 cup distilled water
- ➢ 1/3 cup olive oil
- ➢ 1/3 cup agave nectar or maple syrup
- ➢ ½ cup chopped cherries or berries of your choice (optional)

Preparation

1. Mix all dry ingredients in a large bowl. Mix all wet ingredients thoroughly in another bowl.
2. Add wet ingredients to the dry ingredients and stir just until mixed.
3. Drop batter into greased muffin tin.
4. Bake at 350 degrees for 15-20 minutes.

Banana-Quinoa Muffins

12 servings
Prep and Cook Time: 35 minutes

> This recipe needs very ripe bananas to make moist muffins.

Ingredients

- ➤ ½ cup quinoa flour
- ➤ ½ cup quinoa flakes
- ➤ 2 Tbsp maple syrup
- ➤ 2 tsp non-aluminum baking powder
- ➤ ½ tsp baking soda
- ➤ ½ tsp sea salt
- ➤ 2 very ripe bananas
- ➤ 1 Tbsp olive oil

Preparation

1. Mix quinoa flour and flakes with dry ingredients.
2. In separate bowl, mix together bananas, and oil. Add wet ingredients to dry ingredients.
3. Pour into greased muffin tins. Fill muffin tins ½ full.
4. Bake 20-25 minutes at 400 degrees.

Hot Quinoa and Apple Breakfast Cereal

5 servings
Prep and Cook Time: 10 minutes

Ingredients

➢ 1 cup quinoa
➢ 2 cups water
➢ ½ cup apples, thinly sliced
➢ 1/3 cup raisins
➢ ½ tsp cinnamon
➢ almond milk or cream (pg 25, 102)
➢ maple syrup

Preparation

1. In a medium-sized bowl, soak the quinoa in cold water for 5 minutes.
2. In a medium saucepan, combine the soaked quinoa and water and bring to a boil.
3. Reduce the heat, simmer and cover for 5 minutes.
4. Add apples, raisins, and cinnamon.
5. Simmer until water is absorbed.
6. Serve with almond milk or cream and sweeten to taste with maple syrup.

Teff Pancakes

2 servings (4 per serving)
Prep and Cook Time: 15 minutes

VARIATION: Try adding berries or apples to the batter.

Ingredients

- ➤ 1 cup cooked Teff
- ➤ 1/4 tsp sea salt
- ➤ 1 cup quinoa flour
- ➤ 1 cup amaranth flour
- ➤ 1 cup spelt flour
- ➤ 1 cup water or enough to make batter
- ➤ 1 Tbsp olive oil
- ➤ 1 Tbsp cooked sea moss

Preparation

1. Mix all ingredients
2. Cook on a hot oiled griddle.

Chapter Four

LUNCH

Plantain Wraps (pg 35)

Super Greens Shake

2 servings
Prep and Cook Time: 10 minutes

This is a fantastic way to get greens and chlorophyll. As well, you can drink it while you're fasting.

Ingredients

➤ 1 avocado
➤ 1 cucumber
➤ 1 tomato
➤ 1 lime (peeled)
➤ 2 scoops of Alkaline Foods Green Food Plus Mix (pg 131)
➤ 1 scoop of fruits (See Alkaline Foods List)
➤ 1/2 cup of blue agave nectar
➤ 6-8 ice cubes

Preparation

Place all ingredients in a blender, and blend well.

Plantain Wraps

3 servings (2 wraps per serving)
Prep and Cook Time: 25 minutes

Ingredients

➤ 2 ripe plantains
➤ 1 recipe of duxcell or quinoa mix (pg 44)

Preparation

1. Peel plantains and cut.
2. Heat up olive oil. Sauté plantains over low medium heat. Cook until golden brown on both sides. Remove from heat.
3. Create circle with plantains (see photo on page 33) and stuff with duxcell or quinoa mix.
4. Place in an oven preheated to 325 degrees, until completely warm.

Quinoa and Coriander Cakes with Tahini Ginger Sauce
4 servings
Prep and Cook Time: 35 minutes

Ingredients

➢ 15 oz cooked quinoa, drained
➢ 1 bunch of scallions (white parts only), chopped
➢ 2 tsp ground cumin
➢ 2 tsp of ground coriander
➢ 1 fresh green chili, seeded and finely chopped
➢ 2 Tbsp chopped fresh cilantro
➢ 2 Tbsp all-quinoa flour
➢ seasoned flour for shaping oil, for shallow frying
➢ sea salt
➢ lime wedges and cilantro for garnish.

Tahini Ginger Sauce
➢ 1 knob of minced ginger
➢ 3 Tbsp of tahini
➢ 1 lime juiced
➢ 4 Tbsp of water

Preparation

1. In a blender process the quinoa, scallions, cumin, and ground coriander until smooth and well mixed.
2. Scraped the mixture into a bowl and stir in the chili, fresh cilantro, and measured flour.
3. Mix well and season with sea salt.
4. Add more flour if the mix is too soft.
5. Chill for 30 minutes before shaping.
6. While the mix is chilling, make the Tahini Ginger Sauce.
7. Mix the tahini, ginger, lime juice and water to make a thin paste. Cook for five minutes.
8. Shape the mix into individual cakes with floured hands.
9. Heat the olive oil in a frying pan and fry the cakes in batches for about 1 minute on each side, until crisp and golden.
10. After frying place on paper towel to drain.
11. Serve with dip and garnish with limes and cilantro.

Spiced Dolmades

16-20 servings (1 per serving)
Prep and Cook Time: 65 minutes

Ingredients

- ➤ 20 vacuumed-packed vine leaves in brine
- ➤ ½ cup black rice
- ➤ 3 Tbsp olive oil
- ➤ 1 small red onion, finely chopped
- ➤ 2/3 cup of almonds or walnuts
- ➤ 2 Tbsp chopped lemongrass
- ➤ 3 Tbsp raisins
- ➤ ½ tsp ground cinnamon
- ➤ 2 tsp lime juice
- ➤ 2 Tbsp tomato puree
- ➤ sea salt

Preparation

1. Rinse the vine leaves well under cold running water, then drain.
2. Bring a saucepan of water to a boil. Add rice and lemongrass.
3. Lower the heat, cover and simmer for 10-20 minutes, until almost cooked. Drain.
4. Heat 2 Tbsp of the olive oil in a frying pan, add the onion and cook until soft. Stir in the nuts, and lightly brown.
5. Add in the raisins and cinnamon, with salt to taste.
6. Stir in the rice and mix well. Leave to cool.
7. Line a saucepan with any damaged vine leaves.
8. Trim the stalks from the remaining leaves and lay them flat.
9. Place a little filling on each. Fold the sides over and roll up each leaf neatly.
10. Place the dolmades side by side in the leaf-lined pan, so that they fit tightly.
11. In a bowl, mix 1 ¼ cups water with the lime juice and tomato puree.
12. Add the remaining olive oil.
13. Pour over the dolmades and place a heatproof plate on top to keep them in place.

Spiced Dolmades *(Continued)*

Preparation *(Continued)*

14. Cover the pan and simmer the dolmades for 1 hour, or until all the liquid has been absorbed and the leaves are tender.
15. Transfer to a platter and serve hot or cold.

Baby Onions and Mushrooms

4 servings
Prep and Cook Time: 55 minutes

Ingredients

- ➢ 1 cup diced butternut squash
- ➢ 12 oz baby red onions
- ➢ ½ cup lime juice
- ➢ 4 Tbsp olive oil
- ➢ 1 tsp coriander seeds, lightly crushed
- ➢ 2 bay leaves
- ➢ pinch of cayenne pepper
- ➢ 1 knuckle of ginger
- ➢ 12 oz button mushrooms
- ➢ 3 plum tomatoes, peeled, seeded, and quartered
- ➢ sea salt to taste
- ➢ 3 Tbsp chopped fresh parsley, to garnish

Preparation

1. Peel the baby onions and trim the tops and roots.
2. Heat 3 Tbsp olive oil in a deep frying pan.
3. Add the butternut squash and onions and cook, stirring occasionally, for about 20 minutes, until the vegetables have browned lightly and are beginning to soften.
4. Add the lime juice, coriander seeds, bay leaves, cayenne, ginger, button mushrooms and tomatoes, with sea salt to taste.
5. Cook, uncovered for 20-30 minutes, until the vegetables are soft and the sauce has thickened.
6. Serve chilled, garnished with olive oil and chopped parsley.

Avocado on Rye Sandwich

1 serving
Prep and Cook Time: 10 minutes

Ingredients

➢ 1 avocado
➢ ½ red onion
➢ 2 romaine lettuce leaves
➢ 1 tsp extra virgin olive oil
➢ pinch of sea salt and pepper
➢ 2 slices Rye bread

Preparation

Slice the avocado, and assemble all items between Rye bread. Season to taste. Enjoy!

Chapter Five

DINNER

Quinoa Pilaf (pg 45)

Mediterranean-style Roasted Vegetables with Arame

2-3 servings
Prep and Cook Time: 55 minutes

> A delicious recipe to entertain in style and surprise your friends!

Ingredients

- ½ cup arame
- 4 baby onions, or 1 medium onion, quartered
- 1 red bell pepper, cut into pieces
- handful of mushrooms, cut in half
- 3 Tbsp extra virgin olive oil
- 3 Tbsp concentrated apple juice (optional)
- 1 Tbsp dry oregano
- 2 bay leaves
- pinch of sea salt
- chopped fresh parsley
- capers

Preparation

1. Rinse the arame under cold water quickly.
2. Soak it in just enough cold water to cover it, for 7 minutes, and then drain well.
3. Heat the oven to 375 degrees.
4. In an oven casserole dish, mix the vegetables, arame and seasonings well.
5. Add a small amount of water to just cover the bottom of the dish.
6. Cover with lid and bake until the vegetables are sweet and tender (approximately 30-35 minutes).
7. Garnish with the capers and parsley, and serve.

Amaranth with Amaranth Leaves Tomato Mushroom Sauce

2 servings
Prep and Cook Time: 50 minutes

Ingredients

- ➢ 1 cup amaranth seed
- ➢ 2 ½ cups water
- ➢ 1 Tbsp olive oil
- ➢ 1 bunch of young amaranth leaves (if available)
- ➢ 2 ripe tomatoes
- ➢ 1/2 pound mushrooms, sliced
- ➢ 1 ½ tsp basil
- ➢ 1 ½ tsp oregano
- ➢ 1 Tbsp onion, minced
- ➢ sea salt to taste

Preparation

1. Add amaranth to boiling water.
2. Bring back to boil, reduce heat, cover and simmer for 18-20 minutes.
3. While amaranth is cooking, stem and wash amaranth leaves, then simmer until tender.
4. Dip tomatoes into boiling water to loosen skin, then peel and chop.
5. Heat oil in a skillet over medium heat
6. Sauté onion for approximately 2 minutes, until translucent.
7. Add tomato, mushrooms, basil, oregano, sea salt, and 1 Tbsp water. Drain and chop amaranth leaves and add to tomato mixture.
8. Cook an additional 10–15 minutes, stirring occasionally.
9. Lightly mash tomato as it is cooking and stir the sauce into the amaranth or spoon it on top.

Quinoa: The Basic Recipe

3 servings (8 oz portions)
Prep and Cook Time: 35 minutes

This light and wholesome grain may be prepared quickly and easily with this basic method.

Ingredients

➤ 2 cups distilled water
➤ 1 cup quinoa

Preparation

1. Rinse quinoa, either by using a mesh strainer or by running fresh water over the quinoa in a pot. Drain excess water.
2. Place quinoa and water in a 1 ½ quart saucepan and bring to a boil. Reduce to a simmer, cover, and cook until all of the water is absorbed (about 15 minutes). You will know that the quinoa is done when all the grains have turned from white to transparent, and the spiral-like germ has separated.

Quinoa Pilaf

6-8 servings
Prep and Cook Time: 25 minutes

> Delicious as a side dish with fish as an transitional food.

> VARIATION: Substitute in your favorite vegetables, from the Alkaline food list, or try cooking the quinoa in seaweed stock or vegetable stock instead of water.

Ingredients

- ➢ 6 cups quinoa, cooked (basic recipe, doubled, pg 44)
- ➢ 1/2 cup red onion, diced
- ➢ 1/4 cup olive oil
- ➢ 1/4 cup green pepper, diced
- ➢ 1 cup almonds, sliced
- ➢ 1/4 cup sweet red pepper, diced
- ➢ 1/4 tsp oregano
- ➢ sea salt to taste

Preparation

1. Sauté chopped vegetables in olive oil until clear, yet crisp. Stir in oregano.
2. Add sautéed vegetables to cooked, hot quinoa, mixing well.
3. Add salt to taste.
4. Dry-roast almonds in a heavy skillet until lightly golden, add almonds and mix.

Quinoa Stir Fry

3-4 servings
Prep and Cook Time: 30 minutes

Ingredients

- ➢ 2 cups quinoa, cooked (pg 44)
- ➢ 2-3 stalks broccoli, chopped
- ➢ 1 cup string beans
- ➢ 3 red onions, chopped
- ➢ 1 cup mushrooms, sliced
- ➢ 1 Tbsp grated ginger
- ➢ 2-3 Tbsp olive oil
- ➢ sea salt to taste

Preparation

1. Stir fry veggies in 2-3 Tbsp olive oil till tender.
2. Add 1 Tbsp maple syrup after veggies are done.
3. Add sea salt to taste.
4. Serve with quinoa.

Baked Quinoa and Mixed Veggies

6-8 servings
Prep and Cook Time: 45 minutes

Ingredients

- 1 cup uncooked quinoa
- ½ cup red onion, diced
- ¼ cup olive oil
- ¼ cup green pepper, diced
- ½ cup fresh basil
- ¼ cup sweet red pepper, diced
- ¼ tsp oregano
- 2 cups string beans
- 4 cups mixed mushrooms
- sea salt to taste

Preparation

1. Add 1 cup quinoa to 2 cups distilled water, bring to a boil.
2. Reduce heat and simmer for 5 minutes.
3. Sauté chopped vegetables in olive oil until clear, yet crisp. Stir in oregano
4. Pour sautéed vegetables inside deep baking pan, then add quinoa on top.
5. Bake 20-25 minutes at 400 degrees.
6. Add salt to taste.

Pasta Reina (Royal Pastina-Stuffed Avocado)

8 servings
Prep and Cook Time: 45 minutes

Ingredients

- ½ cup uncooked quinoa
- 1 cup vegetable stock (broth) (pg 95)
- 1 tsp grated lime peel
- 2 Tbsp fresh lime juice
- 2 tsp olive oil
- 3 Tbsp finely chopped red onion
- 6 cherry tomato
- 3 Tbsp finely chopped red bell pepper
- 2 Tbsp chopped fresh cilantro leaves
- ¼ tsp each sea salt and black pepper
- 4 ripe avocados
- 4 cups mixed baby greens
- 2 Tbsp olive oil
- 1 Tbsp lime juice

Preparation

1. In small saucepan over medium-high heat, bring veggie broth and saffron to a boil. Stir in quinoa. Reduce heat to low, cover and cook for 20 minutes.
2. In small bowl combine lime peel and juice, oil, onion, tomato, bell pepper, cilantro, salt, and pepper. Toss with quinoa.
3. Cover and refrigerate for 30 minutes. Just before serving cut avocados in half and remove seed from each.
4. Fill each avocado with quinoa mixture. Whisk olive oil and lime juice and lightly toss salad greens.
5. Arrange 1/2 cup dressed greens on each plate and top with stuffed avocado to serve.

Pizza
Yields 1 pizza
Prep and Cook Time: 10 minutes

Ingredients

➢ pizza sauce (pg 105)
➢ almond cheese/mayo (pg 100, pg 101)
➢ pizza crust

CHOOSE ANY TOPPINGS FROM:

➢ shredded/julienne zucchini
➢ jicama
➢ shredded cabbage
➢ romaine lettuce
➢ minced raw bell peppers
➢ red onions
➢ fresh basil

Preparation

1. Place crust on counter and spread with a thick layer of Almond Cheese/Mayo.
2. Spread a thick layer of pizza sauce, and add toppings. Serve immediately.

Spelt Burgers

4 servings
Prep and Cook Time: 30 minutes

Ingredients

- ➢ 1 cup spelt kernels
- ➢ 1 Tbsp olive oil
- ➢ 1/4 cup chopped onion
- ➢ 2 cups vegetable stock (broth) (pg 95)
- ➢ 2 Tbsp tomato paste
- ➢ 1/4 cup olive oil
- ➢ 1/4 cup almond mayonnaise (pg 101)
- ➢ 4 lettuce leaves
- ➢ 4 slices onion
- ➢ 4 slices tomato
- ➢ 1 cup duxcell
- ➢ 2 Tbsp Irish Moss jelly (pg 99)

Preparation

1. Preheat the oven to 350 degrees.
2. Place the spelt kernels in a blender, and process at medium speed for 2 minutes. Set aside.
3. Heat 1 Tbsp olive oil in a 3-quart saucepan, on medium heat.
4. Add the onion and cook, stirring often, until it's tender but firm.
5. Add the stock and the ground kernels, and mix well.
6. Increase the heat to high, and bring the mixture to a boil.
7. Pour the vegetable mixture into a 2-quart casserole dish, and cover with aluminum foil.
8. Bake for 20 minutes, or until the mixture is sticky and has the consistency of cooked white rice.
9. Cool the mixture to room temperature.
10. Then add tomato paste to taste, and stir to mix.   Using wet hands form the mixture into 4 patties. If the mixture does not hold together well, add the sea moss jelly and mix well before forming the patties.
11. Place the oil in a nonstick 10-inch skillet, and cook the patties over medium heat for 5 to 7 minutes on each side, or until browned and crisp.
12. Transfer the patties to paper towels, to drain.

Spelt Burgers *(Continued)*

Preparation *(Continued)*

13. Cut each Spelt Bun in half. Spread the bottom half of each bun with tomato paste and almond mayonnaise, and top with a leaf of lettuce and a slice of onion.
14. Follow with a drained patty, a slice of tomato, and a few pickle slices. Replace the top of the bun, and serve immediately.

Vegetable Plantain Lasagna with Arame

6-8 servings
Prep and Cook Time: 30 minutes

Ingredients

➤ 1 cup arame sea vegetable
➤ 3 medium leeks, thinly sliced
➤ 2 Tbsp extra virgin olive oil
➤ pinch of sea salt
➤ 2 bay leaves
➤ 6 plantains, sliced thin
➤ 2 cups of diced butternut squash
➤ 1/2 red onion, diced small
➤ 1 cup mushrooms, finely slice
➤ 2 cups of pizza sauce (pg 105)
➤ 1/2 cup almond powder
➤ chopped fresh parsley

Preparation

1. Rinse the arame quickly under cold water; soak with just enough cold water to cover for 5-7 minutes, and drain.
2. Sauté the leeks with the olive oil, pinch of sea salt and the bay leaves for 2-3 minutes.
3. Add the squash, red onion and mushrooms, toss, cover and cook for 12 minutes.
4. Add the arame and a pinch of sea salt and mix well.
5. Cook the plantains in salted boiling water until tender.
6. Rinse under cold water and drain well.
7. Place alternative layers of plantains, vegetable mixture, and tomato sauce, starting and finishing with the plantains.
8. Cover the top layer with more tomato sauce and sprinkle with a generous amount of almond powder.
9. Bake at 375 degrees until golden and crispy. Serve garnished with chopped fresh parsley.

Wild Rice Pilaf

6 servings
Prep and Cook Time: 1 hour and 45 minutes

> If you're looking for rice pilaf for a special occasion, this recipe is for you. It is substantial, full of flavor, and quite easy to prepare. The flavors blend beautifully, and the variety of ingredients make for a highly nutritious dish.

Ingredients

- ½ cup wild rice
- 1 cup long grain black rice
- 1 med onion, chopped
- 2 cups sliced crimini mushrooms
- 1 med green apple, diced about ¼ inch pieces
- ½ cup chopped walnuts
- 6 dried apricots, coarsely chopped
- ½ cup raisins
- ½ cup chopped fresh parsley
- 2 Tbsp chopped fresh sage
- 3 Tbsp chopped fresh thyme
- ½ Tbsp fennel seeds
- ¾ cup + 1 Tbsp vegetable stock (broth) (pg 95)
- 2 Tbsp olive oil
- sea salt and black pepper to taste

Preparation

1. Bring 3½ cups of lightly salted water to a boil. While water is coming to a boil, rinse the wild rice under running water in a strainer.
2. When water is boiling; add both wild and black rice or quinoa, cover, turn heat to low and cook for about 45 minutes, until tender. *Do not overcook*. You will most likely have excess water when rice is cooked properly.
3. Put cooked rice in a strainer and drain out excess water.

Wild Rice Pilaf

Preparation *(Continued)*

4. Heat 1 Tbsp of broth in a large stainless steel skillet. Sauté onion in broth over medium heat for 5 minutes. Add mushrooms and continue to sauté for another 2-3 minutes.
5. Mix all the stuffing ingredients together in bowl and season with sea salt and pepper. Preheat oven to 350 degrees. Place stuffing in an 8-inch square baking dish and bake covered for about 1 hour.
6. Drizzle with olive oil and mix with a fork, to keep it fluffy.

Tomato and Rosemary Spelt Pasta

4 servings
Prep and Cook Time: 25 minutes

Ingredients

- 1 1/2 Tbsp vegetable oil
- 1/2 onion, diced
- 1/4 pound mushrooms, diced
- 1/4 green bell pepper, seeded and diced
- 1 cup diced fresh tomatoes
- 1 1/2 tsp dried rosemary
- sea salt and black pepper to taste
- 2 Tbsp tomato paste
- 2 cups vegetable stock (broth) (pg 95)
- 8 ounces uncooked spelt spaghetti

Preparation

1. Heat the oil in a skillet over the medium heat, and cook until tender.
2. Mix in mushrooms, green bell pepper, and tomatoes. Season with rosemary, sea salt and pepper.
3. Stir in tomato paste and veggie broth.
4. Reduce heat to low, cover and simmer 15 minutes.
5. Bring a large pot of lightly salted water to a boil.
6. Add spelt spaghetti and cook for 8 to 10 minutes or until al dente; drain.
7. Serve sauce over the cooked pasta.

Dried Fruit and Almond Stuffing

Yields 1 pint
Prep and Cook Time: 10 minutes

Ingredients

- 2 Tbsp olive oil
- 1 chopped red onion
- 1 ½ tsp ground cinnamon
- ½ tsp ground cumin
- 1 ½ cup dried fruit (check foods list), soaked for several hours in water
- ¼ cup blanched almonds, chopped
- sea salt to taste

Preparation

1. In a saucepan heat the olive oil. Add the onion and cook gently for 5 minutes until soft.
2. Add the ground cinnamon and cumin and cook, stirring for 2 minutes.
3. Drain the dried fruit, roughly chop, and then add to the onions with the almonds.
4. Season with sea salt to taste, and then serve as desired.

Quinoa and Cumin Stuffing

Yields 1 quart
Prep and Cook Time: 40 minutes

Ingredients

- ½ cup quinoa
- 2 Tbsp olive oil
- 1 small red onion, finely chopped
- 1 tsp ground cinnamon
- 1 tsp ground cumin
- ¾ cup chopped dried apricots, chopped
- ¾ cup chopped walnuts

Preparation

1. Soak the quinoa in warm water for ½ hours, then drain.
2. In a saucepan heat the oil, add the onion and cook until soft.
3. Stir in the cinnamon, cumin, apricots and walnuts, with sea salt to taste. Use as desired.

Quinoa and Wild Rice Dressing

6-8 servings
Prep and Cook Time: 40 minutes

Ingredients

- 5 cups cooked quinoa (pg 44)
- ½ cup scallions, chopped
- 2 cups cooked wild rice
- ½ cup walnuts
- 1 cup mushrooms, sliced
- 1 red onion, chopped
- 1 Tbsp sage, rubbed
- 1 tsp rosemary
- ½ cup parsley, chopped
- 1 tsp thyme
- ¼ cup olive oil
- sea salt and pepper to taste

Preparation

1. In ¼ cup olive oil sauté onion, scallions, parsley, sage, rosemary, and thyme.
2. Add mushrooms and walnuts and toss with quinoa and wild rice.
3. Bake at 350 degrees for 30 minutes.

Calabacitas (Mexican Vegetable Side Dish)

4 servings
Prep and Cook Time: 20 minutes

Calabacitas is a Southwestern vegetable dish that is traditionally made when all the summer squash and green chilies are in season. This recipe combines these delicious ingredients in a healthier way than tradition prescribes, using sautéing, instead of frying.

Ingredients

> 1 medium onion cut in half and sliced thin
> 2 cups zucchini diced in ½ inch cubes
> 2 cups yellow squash, diced in ½ inch cubes
> 15 oz diced cherry tomatoes, drained
> 4 oz diced green chili
> 3 Tbsp + 1 Tbsp vegetable stock (broth) (pg 95)
> ¼ cup chopped cilantro
> 3 Tbsp fresh chopped fresh oregano
> sea salt and black pepper to taste

Preparation

1. Heat 1 Tbsp broth in 11-12 inch stainless steel skillet. Sauté onions in broth over medium heat for about 5 minutes stirring frequently, until translucent. Add zucchini, yellow squash, remaining broth, green chili, and cook for another 10 minutes or so until vegetables are tender, stirring often.
2. Add tomatoes and continue to cook for another couple of minutes. Stir in herbs, salt and pepper. Optional: drizzle with olive oil before serving.

Mediterranean Kale

4 servings
Prep and Cook Time: 15 minutes

Some new varieties of kale are milder tasting. Try it this way; you'll be
pleasantly surprised.

Ingredients

- 2 medium bunches kale, chopped about 12 cups
- 2 Tbsp lime juice
- 1 chopped red onion
- olive oil to taste
- sea salt to taste

Preparation

1. Bring lightly salted water to a boil in a steamer with a tight fitting lid. The
   salt helps to enhance flavor and color of vegetables.
2. While water is coming to a boil, fold each kale leaf in half and pull or cut
   out stem.
3. Chop leaf and rinse in colander. When water comes to a boil, add kale to
   steamer basket and cover. Steam for 7-10 minutes, until tender. Toss
   with rest of ingredients, and serve.

Sautéed Greens

2 servings
Prep and Cook Time: 30 minutes

The leeks are a delicious complement. Adding the oil at the end gives it a rich taste without heating it, making this even healthier than most sautéed greens.

Ingredients

- 1 cup sliced leeks (about 1 leek)
- 4 cups chopped kale
- 1/4 cup + 1 Tbsp vegetable stock (broth) (pg 95)
- 1 tsp fresh lime juice
- 1 red onion
- 1 tsp extra virgin olive oil
- sea salt to taste

Preparation

1. Heat 1 Tbsp broth in a 10-12 inch stainless steel skillet.
2. Sauté sliced leeks in broth over medium low heat for about 5 minutes, stirring frequently.
3. Add kale and ¼ cup broth. Cover and simmer on low heat for about 7-8 minutes, stirring occasionally.
4. Toss with red onion, lime juice, olive oil, sea salt and pepper.

Chapter Six

SALADS AND SOUPS

Tomato Dandelion Salad (pg 65)

Mixed Salad with Arame & Almond Dressing

2-3 servings
Prep and Cook Time: 20 minutes

Here's a quick and simple way to integrate arame into your daily salads.

Ingredients

➤ ½ cup arame
➤ shredded lettuce, to taste
➤ ½ cucumber cut in cubes
➤ 2 Tbsp orange rind
➤ ½ cup almond powder
➤ 2 cups of almond milk (pg 25)
➤ 2 Tbsp extra virgin olive oil

Preparation

1. Quickly rinse the arame under cold water. Then soak it in cold water, cover for 10 minutes, and drain.
2. Mix all the salad ingredients, including the drained arame, in a large serving bowl.
3. Blend the dressing ingredients with a small amount of water to the desired consistency, and serve it with the salad.

Hijiki Salad

2 servings
Prep and Cook Time: 50 minutes

> This sea vegetable is high in calcium, iron, iodine, vitamin B2 and niacin.
> It helps regulate blood sugar levels and has virtually no calories.

Ingredients

➤ 1 cup dry hijiki
➤ pinch sea salt
➤ 1 cup scallions, sliced diagonally
➤ 4 Tbsp roasted un-hulled sesame seeds
➤ 2 tsp lime juice
➤ 1 tsp ginger juice
➤ 2 stalks scallions, thinly cut on the diagonal
➤ olive oil for sautéing

Preparation

1. Quickly rinse the hijiki. Place in a bowl and cover with water.
2. Soak 10 minutes. Place in a saucepan with the soaking water and simmer for 15-20 minutes.
3. Drain, cool and cut into 2" pieces.
4. Reserve soaking water for soup stock or feed it to your plants.
5. Sauté hijiki with sea salt for one minute. Add about 1/3 cup of soaking water, ½ cup of the scallions and cook for a few minutes until liquid has evaporated. Transfer to a serving bowl.
6. Add remaining scallions and sesame seeds.
7. Add enough of the dressing (lime juice and ginger) to saturate the salad and toss.
8. Allow to marinate for 30 minutes before serving.

Tomato Dandelion Salad

2 servings
Prep and Cook Time: 20 minutes

This salad is especially good when tomatoes are in season and vine ripened. Make sure you use young tender dandelion greens, if available.

Ingredients

➤ ½ medium sized onion cut in half and sliced thin
➤ 2 Tbsp lime juice
➤ 1 cup hot water
➤ 1 container of cherry tomatoes
➤ 3 cups chopped young dandelion greens
➤ 2 Tbsp fresh basil cut into large pieces

Preparation

1. Thinly slice the onion and place in a small bowl.
2. Pour 2 Tbsp lime juice and 1 cup hot water over onions and marinate while making rest of salad.
3. Whisk together dressing ingredients, adding oil at the end, a little at a time.
4. Rinse and chop dandelion greens. Place in basket of a salad spinner, rinse and spin dry. Toss dandelion greens with 2/3 of the dressing.
5. Cut tomatoes in half crosswise and squeeze out juice. Cut into quarters, remove inner pulp and slice. Place on greens.
6. Squeeze dry the marinated onions and lay on top of sliced tomatoes and greens.
7. Drizzle the rest of the dressing over tomatoes and onions.
8. Top with basil.

Arame with Smoked Mushrooms and String Beans

2 servings
Prep and Cook Time: 60 minutes

Sensuous, sweet and crunchy!

Ingredients

> 2 Tbsp plus a few drops olive oil
> ½ cup smoked mushrooms, cut into small cubes
> 1 cup arame
> 4 medium red onions cut into thin half moons
> pinch sea salt
> ½ cup water
> ½ cup string beans
> 2 Tbsp apple juice concentrate
> sliced spring onions to garnish

Preparation

1. Heat 2 Tbsp olive oil in a frying pan, add the smoked mushrooms, and gently fry until golden.
2. Remove and drain on a paper towel. Quickly rinse the arame under cold water.
3. Soak mushrooms with just enough cold water to cover them, for 10 minutes, then drain.
4. In the same frying pan, add a few drops of olive oil, the red onions and a pinch of sea salt.
5. Sauté uncovered at medium flame for 10 minutes.
6. Add the water, string beans and arame, cover and cook gently for 20 minutes.
7. Season with the apple juice concentrate and uncover to allow the remaining liquid to evaporate.
8. Mix in the mushrooms and spring onions and serve.

Tabouli

4 servings
Prep and Cook Time: 80 minutes

> Tabouli is a Middle-Eastern salad—try it with quinoa for a delightful new taste.

Ingredients

- ➤ 2 cups quinoa, cooked (pg 44)
- ➤ ½ tsp basil
- ➤ 1 cup chopped parsley
- ➤ ½ cup lime juice
- ➤ ½ cup chopped scallions
- ➤ 1/4 cup olive oil
- ➤ sea salt and pepper to taste
- ➤ 1 Tbsp fresh cilantro lettuce leaves
- ➤ 1/4 cup whole olives, sliced

Preparation

1. Place all ingredients except lettuce and olives in a mixing bowl and toss together lightly.
2. Chill for 1 hour or more to allow flavors to blend.
3. Wash and dry lettuce leaves and use them to line a salad bowl.
4. Add tabouli and garnish with olives.

Seaweed Salad

2-4 servings
Prep and Cook Time: 20 minutes

Ingredients

- ➤ 3/4 oz dried wakame seaweed (whole or cut)
- ➤ 3 Tbsp lime juice
- ➤ 2 Tbsp olive oil
- ➤ 1 tsp maple sugar
- ➤ 1 tsp finely grated peeled fresh ginger
- ➤ 1 small sugar apple
- ➤ 2 scallions, thinly sliced
- ➤ 2 Tbsp chopped fresh cilantro
- ➤ 1 Tbsp sesame seeds, toasted

Preparation

1. Soak seaweed in warm water, 5 minutes.
2. Drain, then squeeze out excess water. If wakame is uncut, cut into ½ - inch-wide strips.
3. Stir together olive oil, maple sugar, ginger, in a bowl until sugar is dissolved.
4. Cut apple into 1/4-inch dice and add to dressing with seaweed, scallions, and cilantro, tossing to combine well.
5. Sprinkle salad with sesame seeds.

Grapes and Apricots Salad

2-4 servings
Prep and Cook Time: 20 minutes

This 10-minute salad is a perfect light, cool dish on a warm day.

Ingredients

- ¾ cup green grapes with seeds
- 3 fresh apricots, cut into eighths
- 3 dried figs, sliced medium thick
- ½ lb mixed salad greens
- 2 Tbsp fresh lime juice
- sea salt and black pepper to taste
- olive oil to taste

Preparation

Toss all ingredients together and serve.

Wild Rice Salad

2 servings
Prep and Cook Time: 35 minutes

Ingredients

- ➢ 4 cups wild rice (presoaked for 48 hours)
- ➢ 2 cucumbers
- ➢ 2 red or green bell peppers
- ➢ 1 small jicama, shredded
- ➢ 1 batch of cherry tomatoes
- ➢ 6 scallions or 1 small red onion
- ➢ 1 cup cilantro, parsley or basil
- ➢ 4 Tbsp kelp, to taste

Dressing

- ➢ 1 large avocado
- ➢ 1/2 to 1 cup tomatillo juice
- ➢ pinch of cayenne
- ➢ kelp to taste
- ➢ cilantro, basil or parsley to taste

Preparation

1. Finely chop all salad ingredients and put into large bowl.
2. Then make the dressing, and drizzle over salad.

Romaine & Avocado Salad

4 servings
Prep and Cook Time: 10 minutes

The light dressing makes this salad lower in fat, without losing flavor.

Ingredients

- 1 large head romaine lettuce, outside leaves discarded
- 1 handful of cherry tomato
- 1 small red bell pepper cut in thin julienned slices, 1 inch long
- 1/2 small avocado cut into chunks
- 2 Tbsp coarsely chopped walnuts, optional

Dressing

- 2 Tbsp lime juice
- olive oil to taste
- sea salt and black pepper to taste

Preparation

1. Cut off tops of lettuce leaves and discard (tops are bitter). Chop remaining inner leaves. Rinse in cold water, and if you have a salad spinner, spin lettuce to dry. If you don't have one, remove as much water as possible in a colander and then dry with paper towels. This will keep the flavor of the salad from getting diluted.
2. Whisk together lime juice, olive oil, sea salt and pepper in a small bowl and toss with salad greens.
3. Sprinkle with chopped walnuts if desired.

Roasted Veggie Green Salad

4 servings
Prep and Cook Time: 40 minutes

This is great when the veggies are still warm from the oven, but you can refrigerate the leftover veggies and use them cold, too. This is best as a salad with only a few veggies.

Ingredients

- lettuce (use several varieties EXCEPT iceberg)
- kale
- green beans
- mushrooms
- red onions
- broccoli,
- dried basil,
- dried cilantro,
- olive oil, other herbs (check food list), as desired

Dressing

- olive oil
- lime juice
- basil

Preparation

1. Chop the veggies into bite-sized pieces. Place them in a large baking pan.
2. Coat the veggies with olive oil and sprinkle them with herbs and sea salt.
3. Mix well to be sure that all of the veggies are coated with olive oil. Put the pan in a 350 degrees oven.
4. Stir the veggies every 15-20 minutes until they are as done as you like them. Put some of the veggies on top of the lettuce mix.
5. For the dressing, mixes 1.5 parts olive oil to 1 part lime juice and add a dash or two of oregano.
6. Mix well and pour over the salad.

Cucumber, Red Onion, and Basil Salad

4 servings
Prep and Cook Time: 20 minutes

Ingredients

- ➢ 2 cucumbers, thinly sliced (about 5 cups)
- ➢ 1/2 red onion, thinly sliced (about 1 ¼ cups)
- ➢ 16 basil leaves, thinly sliced
- ➢ 2 Tbsp lime juice
- ➢ 2 Tbsp olive oil
- ➢ 1/2 tsp sea salt
- ➢ 1/2 tsp white pepper

Preparation

1. Combine all ingredients in a large bowl.
2. Cover and chill for 1 hour.

Cucumber Seaweed Salad

2 servings
Prep and Cook Time: 20 minutes

Ingredients

> 1 Tbsp dried hijiki seaweed
> 3 cups cucumber, peeled, seeds scooped out and sliced
> 1 medium tomato, seeds and excess pulp removed, sliced
> 1 Tbsp minced scallion green or red onions

Dressing

> 3 Tbsp lime juice
> 1/2 Tbsp finely minced fresh ginger
> 1/2 Tbsp chopped fresh cilantro
> olive oil to taste
> sea salt and white pepper to taste

Preparation

1. Rinse and soak hijiki in warm water while preparing rest of ingredients.
2. Peel cucumber and cut in half lengthwise. Scoop out seeds with a small spoon and slice thin.
3. Cut tomato in half crosswise and squeeze out seeds. Quarter and cut out excess pulp. Cut into slices about ¼ inch wide.
4. Whisk the rest of the ingredients together. Squeeze out excess water from seaweed. Chop if necessary. You don't want hijiki pieces to be too large.
5. Toss everything together and serve immediately.

Orange and Red Onion Salad with Cumin

6 servings
Prep and Cook Time: 2 hours

Ingredients

- ➢ 6 oranges
- ➢ 2 red onions
- ➢ 1 Tbsp cumin seeds
- ➢ 1 Tbsp chopped basil
- ➢ 6 Tbsp olive oil
- ➢ sea salt
- ➢ fresh cut basil and olive for garnish

Preparation

1. Slice the oranges thinly, working over a bowl to catch any juice. Then, holding each orange slice, cut the peel and the pith, remove all seeds.
2. Slice the onions thinly and separate the rings.
3. Arrange the orange and onion slices in layers in a shallow dish, sprinkling each layer with cumin seeds, sea salt, basil, and olive oil.
4. Pour over the orange juice left over from slicing the oranges.
5. Leave the salad to marinate in a cool place for about 1 ½ to 2 hours.
6. Garnish with chopped olives then fresh basil then serve.

Cherry Tomatoes Avocado Style

2-4 servings
Prep and Cook Time: 20 minutes

This is a great appetizer, or it could be served as a salad course.

Ingredients

➤ 1 pint cherry tomatoes
➤ Juice from ½ lime
➤ 1 avocado
➤ ½ Tbsp minced cilantro
➤ 1/8 tsp Alkaline Foods seasoning (pg 93, use more if you like extra spice)
➤ 1/8 tsp sea salt

Preparation

1. Slice tomatoes into halves.
2. Drain on paper towels upside down.
3. In Cuisinart with an S blade, add remaining ingredients and pulse chop into a well-mixed chunky consistency.
4. Place tomatoes in bowl, and add avocado mixture on top.

Avocado Soup

6-8 servings
Prep and Cook Time: 30 minutes

Ingredients

- ½ cup minced onion
- 1 Tbsp olive oil
- 1 (15½ oz) can diced cherry tomatoes in juice
- 1 ½ quarts vegetable stock (broth) (pg 95)
- ¼ cup coarsely chopped cilantro leaves
- ½ tsp sea salt
- pinch red pepper
- 2 large ripe avocadoes, cubed

Preparation

1. In skillet, sauté onion in oil 1 to 2 minutes or until onion is transparent.
2. Blend sautéed onion with tomatoes in juice for 30 to 45 seconds in blender.
3. In a stockpot combine puree mixture, veggie broth, cilantro, sea salt, and red pepper.
4. Bring to a boil, reduce heat and simmer 10 minutes longer.
5. Ladle hot soup into bowls, garnish with avocado and lime juice to taste.

Chilled Avocado Soup

2-4 servings
Prep and Cook Time: 20-60 minutes

Ingredients

➤ 4 large avocados (about 2 pounds)
➤ Juice of 1 lime
➤ 1 pint chilled vegetable stock (pg 95)
➤ sea salt and black pepper

Preparation

1. All ingredients should be chilled at all times. Avocado will discolor if left standing too long. You can serve immediately or chill for a short time in the refrigerator.
2. Peel and slice avocado.
3. Mix with lime juice. Put into food processor with vegetable stock.
4. Blend until it forms a puree.
5. Blend until smooth. Test to see if soup is cool enough. If not, chill for 1 to 1 ½ hours, but not more.

Portabella Mushroom Seaweed Soup

4 servings
Prep and Cook Time: 45 minutes

The combination of vegetables and portabella mushrooms gives your body a great dose of minerals in a delicious and easy way.

Ingredients

- ➤ 6 whole dried medium portabella mushrooms
- ➤ 6 cups warm water
- ➤ 4 medium sized pieces wakame seaweed
- ➤ 2 Tbsp chopped dulse seaweed
- ➤ 1 medium onion, quartered and sliced thin
- ➤ 2 Tbsp minced fresh ginger
- ➤ 2 Tbsp vegetable stock (broth) (pg 95)
- ➤ 1 Tbsp lime juice
- ➤ 3 Tbsp minced scallion greens for garnish
- ➤ sea salt and white pepper to taste

Preparation

1. Rinse mushrooms and wakame and soak in 2 cups of warm water for about 10 minutes, or until soft. Save water.
2. Heat 1 Tbsp seaweed water in medium sized soup pot. Sautee onion in seaweed water over medium heat for about 5 minutes, stirring frequently.
3. Add ginger and continue to sauté for another minute.
4. When mushrooms and wakame are soft, slice the mushrooms thinly, and chop the seaweed. Cut out stems when slicing mushrooms and discard. Add to soup pot along with soaking water, and 4 more cups of water.
5. Bring to a boil on high heat.
6. Add dulse. Once it comes to a boil, reduce heat to medium and simmer uncovered for about 10 minutes.
7. Season with sea salt, pepper, and lime juice.
8. Add minced scallion and serve.

Chilled Tomato Basil Soup

4 servings
Prep and Cook Time: 40 minutes

You can use more or less basil according to your own taste.

Ingredients

➤ 2 ½ pounds ripe cherry tomatoes
➤ 2 large bunches fresh basil - reserved a few leaves for garnish
➤ 2 cups vegetable stock (broth) (pg 95)
➤ 2 Tbsp olive oil
➤ 2 Tbsp natural red wine
➤ 1/2 Tbsp lime juice
➤ sea salt and black pepper to taste

Preparation

1. Place tomatoes in food processor in batches and puree.
2. Add the puree to a saucepan with veggie stock.
3. Puree basil with olive oil in the food processor.
4. Add to the saucepan. Simmer for 20 minutes. Remove from heat and let cool.
5. When cool enough to work with, pass the soup through the fine blade of a food mill, or push through a sieve.
6. Put in refrigerator to chill.

Golden Squash Soup

4-6 servings
Prep and Cook Time: 30 minutes

This soup will surprise you. There is just enough coconut milk in it to make it rich tasting and creamy without being high in fat. It is a perfect soup recipe for those days when you want something warm and comforting.

Ingredients

- 1 medium sized butternut squash, peeled and cut into about ½ inch pieces (about 3 cups)
- 1 large red onion, chopped
- 1 Tbsp chopped fresh ginger
- 1 tsp tumeric
- 2 ¾ cups + 1 Tbsp vegetable stock (broth) (pg 95)
- 6 oz canned coconut milk
- 2 Tbsp chopped fresh cilantro
- sea salt and white pepper to taste

Preparation

1. Heat 1 Tbsp broth in medium soup pot. Sauté onion in broth over medium heat for about 5 minutes, stirring frequently, until translucent.
2. Add ginger, and continue to sauté for another minute.
3. Add turmeric, and mix well. Add squash and broth, and mix. Bring to a boil on high heat. Once it comes to a boil reduce heat to medium low and simmer uncovered until squash is tender, about 10 minutes.
4. Place in blender and blend with coconut milk. Make sure you blend in batches, filling blender only half full. Start on low speed, so hot soup does not erupt and burn you.
5. Blend until smooth, about 1 minute. Thin with a little broth if needed.
6. Season to taste with sea salt and white pepper.
7. Reheat, and add cilantro to garnish.

Hot and Sour Soup

6 servings
Prep and Cook Time: 40 minutes

Ingredients

- ➢ 2 lemongrass stalks
- ➢ 6 ¼ cups vegetable stock (broth) (pg 95)
- ➢ 4 lime leaves
- ➢ 2 slices peeled fresh ginger root
- ➢ 6 Tbsp fresh lime juice
- ➢ 6 scallions chopped
- ➢ 1 fresh red chili, seeded and cut into thin strips

- ➢ 1 ¾ cups of oyster mushrooms sliced
- ➢ fresh cilantro leaves and lime slices to garnish

Preparation

1. Lightly crush the lemongrass and add the stalks to a pan with the stock, lime leaves and ginger.
2. Bring to a boil, lower the heat and simmer for 20 minutes.
3. Strain the stock into a clean pan and discard the aromatics.
4. Add the lime juice, scallions, chili and mushrooms.
5. Bring to a boil, lower the heat and simmer for 5 minutes.
6. Serve, garnish with cilantro leaves and lime slices.

Lemongrass Soup

4 servings
Prep and Cook Time: 50 minutes

Ingredients

➤ 8 cups seaweed soup stock (pg 96)
➤ ½ - 1 bunch cilantro
➤ 1 can straw mushrooms
➤ juice of 1 lime
➤ ½ - 1 tsp crushed red pepper
➤ 1 chili pepper, cut into rings
➤ a few stalks of lemongrass, approximately 6

Preparation

1. Bring the broth to a simmer.
2. Add crushed red pepper.
3. Simmer for 5 min. Add lemongrass and simmer for another 5 min.
4. Add the rest of the ingredients and simmer a few minutes more.
5. Be careful not to overcook, or to let the vegetables lose their color or get limp.

Lemongrass and Coconut Cream Soup

6 servings
Prep and Cook Time: 45 minutes

Ingredients

- 1 bunch scallion chopped
- 2 lemongrass stalks, chopped
- 6 lime leaves, chopped
- 7 fl oz coconut cream
- 2 Tbsp chopped fresh cilantro
- ½ cup water
- sea salt to taste

Preparation

1. In a large saucepan, sauté scallions, lemongrass, and lime leaves. Simmer until the water has almost evaporated.
2. Stir in the coconut cream and cilantro, with sea salt to taste.

Watermelon Soup

4 servings
Prep and Cook Time: 20 minutes

Ingredients

➤ 6 cups of very cold watermelon juice made from ripe, chilled seeded watermelon (use juicer)
➤ 1/2 tsp rose water, optional
➤ 1 pinch sea salt
➤ chilled watermelon balls for garnish

Preparation

1. Combine all the ingredients except the garnish and chill deeply.
2. Serve in large chilled goblets and top with garnish.

Watermelon and Ginger Soup

4 servings
Prep and Cook Time: 20 minutes

Ingredients

- ➤ 5 cups of watermelon
- ➤ 2 cups of mango
- ➤ 1/4 cup of lime juice
- ➤ 1 Tbsp fresh ginger
- ➤ 1 Tbsp agave nectar
- ➤ 1/8 tsp ground cardamom

Preparation

1. Place 1 ½ cups of watermelon and 1 cup of mango in food processor and chop into nice sized chunks.
2. Pour into a giant bowl.
3. Place the remaining mango and watermelon in food processor.
4. Add in the remaining ingredients, and blend until liquefied/pureed.
5. Pour that into the giant bowl, and mix.

Watermelon Gazpacho Soup

2 servings
Prep and Cook Time: 20 minutes

Ingredients

- ➤ 2 ½ cups fresh watermelon juice (use juicer)
- ➤ 2 tomatoes chopped
- ➤ 1 small cucumber peeled and diced
- ➤ 3 scallions salt and pepper

Preparation

1. In a blender combine watermelon juice, tomatoes, cucumber, scallions.
2. Add salt and pepper. Serve in bowls.

Mixed Melon Soup

2 servings
Prep and Cook Time: 65 minutes

Ingredients

- ➤ 1 ½ cups honeydew melon, cantaloupe melon and watermelon, cut in chunks
- ➤ 1 Tbsp pickled ginger, chopped
- ➤ sea salt to taste
- ➤ pinch cayenne pepper
- ➤ 1 Tbsp fresh lime juice

Preparation

1. Place honeydew melon, cantaloupe melon and watermelon chunks, pickled ginger, and lime juice in a food processor and process until smooth.
2. Pour into a large bowl and refrigerate for at least 1 hour.

Chapter Seven

DRESSINGS, SAUCES AND CONDIMENTS

Papaya Salsa (pg.107)

Tomato Cucumber Dressing

Yields 1.5 cups
Prep and Cook Time: 5 minutes

Ingredients

- 1 batch of cherry tomatoes chopped
- 1 Tbsp fresh oregano, minced
- 1 cucumber, chopped
- 3 Tbsp sweet basil, chopped
- 1 cup of olive oil
- sea salt to taste

Preparation

Place the above ingredients in blender and process until smooth.

Basil and Tomato Dressing

Yields 1.5 cups
Prep and Cook Time: 5 minutes

Try this dressing with your favorite grains from the alkaline food list, like black rice or quinoa, as well as on your salads or vegetable dishes.

Ingredients

➢ 1 batch of cherry tomatoes
➢ small bunch of basil
➢ juice of one slice of lime
➢ spring or distilled water
➢ sea salt to taste

Preparation

Blend all ingredients in blender. Add water to achieve desired consistency.

Sweet Basil Dressing

Yields 1.5 cups
Prep and Cook Time: 5 minutes

Enjoy!

Ingredients

- 1 cup roughly chopped fresh basil leaves
- 2/3 cup olive oil
- 3 Tbsp water
- 2 tsp maple syrup
- 3½ Tbsp freshly squeezed lime juice
- sea salt and black pepper, to taste

Preparation

Blend all ingredients in a blender or food processor until creamy.

Dry Seasoning

Yields 3 oz
Prep and Cook Time: 20 minutes

This seasoning is also good sprinkled on top of salads for extra flavor.

Ingredients

- 1 Tbsp dehydrated onion flakes
- ½ tsp sweet dry basil
- 1 Tbsp oregano
- 1 Tbsp kelp
- 1 Tbsp dulse
- 1 Tbsp sea salt

Preparation

1. Grind in seed mill or blender until it reaches a powder consistency.
2. Store in sealed glass jar in cool, dry place.

Sea Lettuce Seasoning

Collect sea lettuce fronds and rinse several times in fresh water. The fronds may be dried slowly by spreading them on newspaper and placing them in the sun or in a warm room for about a week. Alternatively, they may be dried for several hours in a warm oven, but the odor of seaweed will permeate the air, and it is not particularly pleasant! After drying, the fronds will be reduced in size and blackened. Crumble them finely and use as a seasoning with rice, soups, and main dishes.

Vegetable Stock

Yields 3 quarts
Prep and Cook Time: 50 minutes

Ingredients

- ➢ 2 bunches of leeks
- ➢ 2 peppers
- ➢ 2 zucchini
- ➢ 2 squash
- ➢ 1 bunch of chives

Preparation

1. In a large stock pot, place cut vegetables with 1 gallon of water.
2. Simmer for 45 minutes and strain. Use stock as a cooking medium.

Seaweed Soup Stock

Yields 1 gallon
Prep and Cook Time: 40 minutes

Edible kelp, Irish moss, and dulse can all be used in this recipe. The resulting soup is clear and can be used as a base.

Ingredients
➤ 8 oz Fresh or dried kelp
➤ 2 oz Fresh or dried Irish moss
➤ 4 oz Fresh or dried dulse
➤ 1 gallon of distilled water

Preparation

1. Clean seaweed by rinsing with fresh water. If edible kelp is used, remove its olive-colored membrane.
2. In a pot, cover seaweed with water and boil for 30 minutes. Serve hot as a soup with added seasonings, or cooled as a jelly.

Mushroom Broth

Yields 1 gallon
Prep and Cook Time: 65 minutes

Ingredients

- 1 pound of mushrooms, sliced
- 1 onion small diced
- thyme, bay leaf, chives, and coriander

Preparation

1. In a stock pot, sauté the onions until translucent.
2. Then add the sliced mushrooms and herbs, and stir.
3. Cook until the mushrooms start to render their liquids, then add 1 gallon of water. Allow to cook slowly for 1 hour. Upon completion, liquid should have a dark brown tone.
4. Allow the cooked mushrooms to drain for an hour, saving the liquid.
5. Then take the drained cooked mushrooms and food process it until finely chopped. These chopped mushrooms can be used in the Duxcell recipe on the following page.

Mushroom Duxcell

4 servings
Prep and Cook Time: 30 minutes

Try over grains, vegetables or pasta. This can also be used as a stuffing.

Ingredients

➤ 1 pound of finely chopped mushrooms (can use leftovers from Mushroom Broth, pg 97)
➤ 2 zucchini, small dice
➤ 2 squash, small dice
➤ 1 red pepper, small dice
➤ 1 cup minced parley
➤ coriander, sea salt, and fresh thyme

Preparation

1. In a large pan, heat olive oil over low heat, and sauté the mushrooms until dry. This process should take about 15 minutes. Stir occasionally, and keep your eye on it.
2. Add the diced zucchini, squash, and red pepper to the mushrooms. Season the mix with coriander, sea salt, fresh thyme, and chopped parley.

Irish Moss Jelly

Yields 1 pint
Prep and Cook Time: 10 minutes

Ingredients

➤ 3 lbs fresh Irish moss
➤ 1 cup maple sugar or syrup (per cup of juice)
➤ juice of half a lime

Preparation

1. Rinse moss in fresh water to remove all traces of salt.
2. Chop fronds into small 1 to 2-inch pieces and place into a saucepan with 2 quarts of boiling water.
3. Cook till water begins to thicken. Remove from heat, strain and measure juice. To each cup of juice add sugar as directed above.
4. Mix together in saucepan and add lime juice. Bring to a boil while stirring constantly.
5. Boil for 1 full minute, and then pour into hot, sterile jars and seal.

Almond Cheese

Yields 1 pint
Prep and Cook Time: 10 minutes

Ingredients

- 2 cups almonds seeds
- 1 cup hulled sesame seeds (soaked)
- 1/2 cup green onions (chopped)
- 1 inch piece ginger (peeled and chopped)
- 1/2 cup parsley
- 1 Tbsp dulse

Preparation

1. Combine all ingredients in blender, add 1 cup of water, cover and blend.
2. Pour into cheese bag and hang in the sink for several hours or overnight to drain.
3. Chill and store in the refrigerator.

Almond Mayo

Yields 1 pint
Prep and Cook Time: 10 minutes

This fluffy, creamy spread is concentrated and rich. Use it in wraps, on pizzas, in fillings, or anywhere you would normally use mayonnaise.

Ingredients

➤ 2 cups soaked almonds, blanched (to blanch, place in boiling water for 30 seconds, cool and pinch off skins. Discard skins.)
➤ 1 lime, juiced
➤ ½ -1 tsp sea salt (to taste)
➤ ¼ cup olive oil

Preparation

1. Mix the lime and sea salt.
2. Place all wet ingredients into food processor. With the food processor running, drop the blanched almonds through the top opening. Blend well and emulsify to a thick, fluffy consistency.
3. Scrape sides and stir if needed. Adjust consistency with water if needed.
4. Refrigerate mixture in an airtight container.

Almond Cream

Yields 1 quart
Prep and Cook Time: 10 minutes

Ingredients

- 2 oz almond flour
- 2 oz olive oil
- 1 quart almond milk

Preparation

1. In a saucepan over medium low heat, heat the olive oil with the almond flour. Stir constantly until oil and flour is well mixed.
2. While stirring add the almond milk, continued to mix until thickened, and season with sea salt.

Pesto Sauce

Yields 1 pint
Prep and Cook Time: 10 minutes

> Try it over tomato and cucumber slices.

Ingredients

- 2 cups fresh basil
- 3/4 cup of extra virgin olive oil
- 2 Tbsp of raw almonds (plump in water for 6 hours)
- sea salt to taste

Preparation

Blend all ingredients in a blender or food processor until creamy.

Guacamole
Yields 1.5 cups
Prep and Cook Time: 10 minutes

Ingredients

- ➤ 5 avocados
- ➤ 10 cherry tomatoes, diced
- ➤ 3 red onions, sliced thin
- ➤ 1-2 tsp dulse seaweed

Preparation

1. Cut the avocado lengthwise, and then twist to open.
2. Remove the pit.
3. Score avocado meat first lengthwise, then across to form crisscross pattern.
4. Scoop out and put into a bowl. Do NOT mash the avocado.
5. Add remaining ingredients and mix gently.

Sauce for Pizza

Yields 1 cup
Prep and Cook Time: 10 minutes

Ingredients

- 2 cartons/packages cherry or grape tomatoes
- 1 Tbsp dried oregano (can use fresh if desired)
- ½ cup sun dried tomatoes (olive oil packed)
- 1/3 cup fresh basil
- ½ tsp sea salt
- 1 tsp – 1 Tbsp sea moss (to thicken sauce, if necessary)

Preparation

Place all ingredients into food processor and pulse chop to chunky consistency.

Tomato Salsa

Yields 1 cup
Prep and Cook Time: 10 minutes

Ingredients

➤ 1 cup fresh chopped tomatoes, add 2 chopped tomatoes
➤ 1/4 cup chopped red onion, add 1 chopped onion
➤ 1/4 cup green pepper, add 1 chopped green pepper
➤ 1/4 tsp cayenne
➤ 1/4 cup fresh cut cilantro

Preparation

1. Blend ingredients in food processor.
2. Add 2 chopped tomatoes, 1 chopped green pepper, and 1 chopped onion to the blended base.
3. Season to taste with dulse, sea salt or more cayenne.

Papaya Salsa

2 servings
Prep and Cook Time: 20 minutes

Ingredients

> 1 papaya
> ½ small red onion, diced
> 1 fresh chili, seeded and finely chopped
> 3 Tbsp chopped fresh cilantro
> grated rind and juice of 1 lime
> sea salt to taste

Preparation

1. Cut the papaya in half and scoop out the seeds.
2. Remove the skin and dice the flesh in small cubs. In a mixing bowl add the papaya, onion, chili, cilantro, limejuice and rind, with sea salt to taste.
3. Mix well, let sit, and serve.

Tomato and Olive Salsa

Yields 1 quart
Prep and Cook Time: 10 minutes

Ingredients

- 1½ cup pitted olives, chopped
- 1 small red onion, small diced
- 4 plumb tomatoes, peeled and small diced
- 1 chili, seeded and finely chopped
- 2 Tbsp olive oil
- ¼ cup fresh basil, chopped.

Preparation

In a bowl, mix all ingredients, season with sea salt and let sit, then serve.

Avocado and Mango Salsa

Yields 1 pint
Prep and Cook Time: 15 minutes

Ingredients

- 1 ripe avocado
- 1 ripe but firm mango
- juice of 1 lime
- 4 scallions, white finely chopped and green cut on a bias
- 1 fresh red chili, seeded and finely chopped
- 2 Tbsp of finely chopped dill

Preparation

1. After the stone has been removed and skin peeled off, dice the avocado.
2. Toss the cut avocado in lime juice so it doesn't oxidize. Do the same with the mango.
3. Mix the mango, avocado, scallion, dill and chili, and season with sea salt to taste.
4. Mix well and cover.

Baba Ganoush

Yields 1 pint
Prep and Cook Time: 50 minutes

Ingredients

- 2 small eggplants
- 4 Tbsp tahini
- ¼ cup ground almonds
- juice of 1 lime
- ½ tsp ground cumin
- 2 Tbsp thyme leaves
- 2 Tbsp of olive oil
- sea salt to taste

Preparation

1. Cut the eggplants in half and roast with olive oil until the flesh is tender.
2. Remove the peel, chop the flesh roughly and leave to drain in a colander.
3. Squeeze out as much liquid from the eggplant as possible.
4. Place the flesh in a blender or food processor. Add the remaining ingredients with sea salt to taste, and process until smooth.

Chapter Eight

DESSERTS

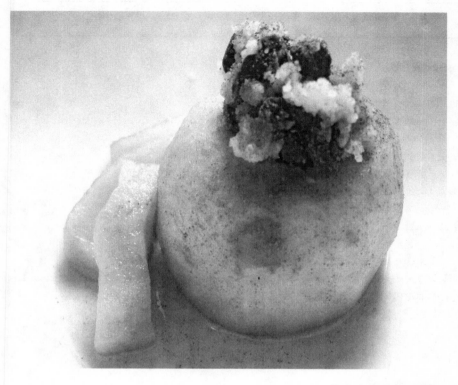

Baked Apple (pg 115)

Teff Almond Cookies

Yields 12-15 cookies
Prep and Cook Time: 45 minutes

VARIATION: Try adding almond nuts or raisins.

Ingredients

- ➢ 3/4 cup quinoa flour
- ➢ 1/4 cup spelt flour
- ➢ 1/4 cup uncooked teff
- ➢ 1/4 cup maple syrup (or agave syrup)
- ➢ 1/2 cup water or almond milk
- ➢ 1/4 tsp almond extract

Preparation

1. Mix dry ingredients. Mix liquids. Combine mixtures.
2. Drop small spoonfuls onto oiled baking sheet. Bake at 350 degrees for 8-10 minutes.

Almond Nut Pie Crust

Yields 1 crust
Prep and Cook Time: 45 minutes

Ingredients

- ½ cup spelt flour
- ½ cup ground almonds
- 1 Tbsp arrowroot powder
- ½ tsp ground cinnamon
- 1/8 tsp ground cloves
- 1/3 cup maple syrup
- 1 tsp Frontier alcohol-free vanilla
- 2 Tbsp water

Preparation

1. Combine dry ingredients in a mixing bowl.
2. Combine the water, vanilla and pour over dry ingredients.
3. Mix well and transfer mixture to a 9" pie plate.
4. Press mixture firmly into place with your fingers, making sure to cover bottom and sides of pie plate.
5. For an unfilled piecrust, bake empty pie shell at 350 degrees for 18-20 minutes or until lightly brown. Cool and fill with pie filling. For a filled pie crust, first bake the empty crust for 10 minutes, then fill and finish baking pie, as per the recipe.

Chilled Peach Soup

4 servings
Prep and Cook Time: 30 minutes

Ingredients

- ➤ 1 quart frozen, sweetened peaches, thawed
- ➤ 1 cup orange juice
- ➤ ¼ lime juice
- ➤ ½ cup peach juice (from thawed peaches)

Preparation

1. Blend peaches in blender.
2. Add remaining ingredients and mix thoroughly.
3. Strain and serve chilled.

Baked Apple

4 servings
Prep and Cook Time: 75 minutes

> If you like apples—and who doesn't—you will love this baked apple recipe. It's even perfect for company.

Ingredients

- 4 crisp red apples
- 2 Tbsp fresh lime juice
- 2 cups water
- ½ cup maple syrup
- ½ cup raisins
- ½ cup chopped walnuts
- 1 tsp cinnamon

Preparation

1. Preheat oven to 350 degrees.
2. Core apples using a melon scooper leaving the bottom of apple so they can hold the stuffing.
3. Combine lime juice and water, and place apples in it as you complete coring them.
4. Mix stuffing ingredients together and fill the cavities of the apples.
5. Place apples in a baking dish with about 1 cup of the lime water in the bottom of the dish.
6. Bake uncovered for about 50-60 minutes depending on size of apples, until they are tender.
7. Drizzle juice from bottom of pan over apples and serve hot.

Apricot Tart

8-10 servings
Prep and Cook Time: 30 minutes; Chilling Time: 1 hour

This easy-to-prepare tart is a wonderful combination of walnuts, dates and apricots, making it a delicious and highly nutritious dessert.

Ingredients

- 2½ cups walnuts
- 1½ cups dates
- 2 cups dried apricots, sliced ¼ inch thick
- 2 Tbsp agave nectar
- 1 cup orange juice
- ½ tsp cinnamon

Preparation

1. Remove pits from dates if they have them and place them in a food processor with walnuts. Process until well mixed and ground, but not smooth, about 40 seconds. It should be a coarsely textured when done.
2. Press evenly into a 9-inch tart pan with about ½ inch crust around rim. Set in refrigerator while making the filling.
3. Slice apricots about ¼ inch thick, and cook in a 10 inch skillet with agave nectar, orange juice and cinnamon on medium low heat, until apricots become tender, and liquid is syrupy, about 10 minutes.
4. Remove apricots and syrup from hot pan and let cool in bowl for about 1 hour so it gets fairly cool.
5. Spread evenly over crust. It can be served right away or chilled. Make sure you store tart covered so it doesn't pick up moisture from the refrigerator.

Watermelon Frappe

2 servings
Prep and Cook Time: 20 minutes

A great alternative to watermelon slices.

Ingredients

- ➤ 4 cups cold watermelon chunks
- ➤ 8 mint leaves

Preparation

1. Run the blender at medium speed and drop chunks of watermelon through the feed whole one at a time until they are well integrated.
2. Add the mint and run the blender at medium speed for 1 minute until the watermelon has liquefied.
3. Strain into a bowl with a pouring lip. Pour into goblets, garnish with a sprig of sorrel and enjoy!

Apricot Compote

Yields 2 cups
Prep and Cook Time: 20 minutes

This easy compote is quick and naturally sweet. It can be served alone, or topped with fresh fruit such as pears or apples.

Ingredients

- 1 cup dried apricots, sliced
- ½ cup raisins
- ½ cup of chopped walnuts
- 2 Tbsp lime juice
- 1 ½ cups orange juice
- 2 Tbsp agave nectar

Preparation

1. Bring the lime juice, orange juice and agave nectar to a boil and add apricots and raisins in a small saucepan.
2. Reduce heat to low and simmer just until they become tender and a little syrupy, about 10 minutes.
3. Do not overcook, or they will dissolve. You want to still have definition in your fruit. Remove apricots and raisins with a slotted spoon and reduce sauce for about 2 minutes to thicken.
4. Remove from heat and add apricots, raisins, and walnuts back to sauce.
5. Serve warm or chilled.

Chicago Ice Cream

Yields 1 gallon
Prep and Cook Time: 90 minutes

Ingredients

- 2 oz Irish moss
- 1 gallon of almond milk see pg 25
- 1 Cup of agave nectar or maple syrup
- 1 cup of mixed fruits

Preparation

1. Irish moss soaked in warm water about an hour, and rinsed well to clear it of a certain foreign taste.
2. Then steep it in almond milk, keeping it just at the point of boiling or simmering for an hour, or until a rich yellow color is given to the milk. and this will do to steep twice.
3. Sweeten with agave nectar or maple syrup.
4. Add mixed fruits.
5. Pour finished mix in a plastic contain with a lid and freeze for 30 minutes, then serve.

Blueberry and Peach Crisp

4-6 servings
Prep and Cook Time: 55 minutes

This crisp is easy to make, and an excellent way to enjoy the nutritional benefits of blueberries in any season.

Ingredients

- 10 oz fresh or frozen blueberries
- 1 lb of fresh or frozen peach slices
- ¼ cup apple juice
- ½ cup almonds
- 1 cup pitted dates
- 2 Tbsp apple juice
- ½ tsp cinnamon

Preparation

1. Preheat oven to 350 degrees.
2. Place blueberries in the bottom of a square, 8-inch baking pan. If you are using frozen fruit, make sure it is completely thawed and drained of excess water.
3. Place peach slices on top of blueberries. If they are frozen make sure they are also thawed and drained of excess water.
4. Drizzle ¼ cup apple juice over fruit.
5. Remove pits from dates and place in the food processor along with cinnamon and almonds. Process for a minute, or until the dates are blended with apple juice.
6. Place mixture evenly over peaches and blueberries, and bake uncovered for about 45 minutes.
7. Serve warm or cool.

Cold Cherry Soup

8 servings
Prep and Cook Time: 20 minutes; Chilling Time: 2 hours

> May be served in a bowl as a cold soup, or in a glass as a beverage.

Ingredients

- ➤ 2 ½ pounds ripe cherries
- ➤ 2 ½ cups granulated agave nectar
- ➤ 2 ½ quarts water
- ➤ juice of ½ lime
- ➤ ¼ tsp ground cinnamon

Preparation

1. Wash and stem cherries. Remove pits. Combine pitted cherries, agave nectar, and water in a pot and heat to boiling.
2. Reduce to simmer for 10 minutes. Using a slotted spoon, remove cherries into a large bowl. Set aside.
3. Add lime juice and cinnamon to cherry juice remaining in pot. Boil for 4 minutes, stirring.
4. Remove from heat, pour over cherries and chill.

Cold Strawberry Soup

1 serving
Prep and Cook Time: 20 minutes

Ingredients

- ➢ 1 Tbsp vanilla extract
- ➢ 1 cup maple sugar
- ➢ 1 pint washed strawberries
- ➢ 1/8 tsp nutmeg
- ➢ ½ tsp cinnamon
- ➢ 2 Tbsp agave nectar

Preparation

1. Blend all ingredients.
2. Serve cold.

Elderberry Jelly

Yields 12 jars
Prep and Cook Time: 45 minutes

The most common use of elderberries is for jelly-making. Their juice produces a clear, ruby-red, jewel-like delicacy with a sparkling flavor to match.

Ingredients

➢ 3 pounds elderberries
➢ juice of 1 lime
➢ 1 box fruit pectin
➢ 4 ½ cups maple sugar

Preparation

1. Heat the berries over a low fire until the juice starts to flow and then simmer the fruit for 15 minutes.
2. Strain the liquid through a double layer of cheesecloth. This is easier if you cook the fruit in the evening and let it drain overnight.
3. Mix the elderberry and lime juices along with just enough water to make three cups of fluid.
4. Add the pectin, bring the mixture to a boil and stir in the maple sugar.
5. Bring the jelly to a full boil again for one minute, pour it into sterilized glasses and cover the jars with paraffin.

Spiced Elderberries

Yields 2-3 quarts
Prep and Cook Time: 45 minutes

Ingredients

- 10 cups ripe elderberries
- 2 cups agave nectar
- 2 tsp ground cinnamon
- ½ tsp allspice
- ½ tsp ground cloves

Preparation

1. Cook the berries about 20 minutes, until they're slightly soft. Stir very frequently while cooking.
2. Add the other ingredients and heat the mixture until it has barely thickened. Test the consistency by dripping some of the solution from a spoon. The juice should divide into drops instead of flowing off in a stream.
3. Pour the fruit into hot, sterilized jars and seal the tops.

Chapter Nine

SOME TRANSITIONAL FOODS

Halibut with Avocado Salsa (pg 126)

Halibut with Avocado Salsa

4 servings
Prep and Cook Time: 20 minutes

Spicy salsa compliments the flavor of halibut for a healthy, quick and easy dinner. The avocado adds rich flavor to the salsa, along with extra vitamins and minerals.

Ingredients

- 4 4-6 oz halibut steaks or filets
- ¼ cup minced scallion
- 1-2 tsp finely minced jalapeno
- ¼ cup + 1 Tbsp fresh lime juice
- 3 Tbsp chopped fresh cilantro
- 8 cherry tomatoes, quartered
- 1 medium ripe but firm avocado diced in ¼ inch cubes
- dulse salt or sea salt and black pepper to taste

Preparation

1. Mix all ingredients except halibut and 1 Tbsp lime in a bowl and set aside.
2. Preheat a 10-12 inch stainless steel skillet on medium high heat for about 2 minutes.
3. Rub halibut with 1 Tbsp lime juice and season with a little sea salt and black pepper.
4. Place in hot pan. You do not need oil or liquid.
5. Cook for about 3 minutes and turn.
6. Cook for another 3 minutes and remove from pan. Place on plate, and top with salsa.

Salmon, Cucumber, Dill Salad

4 servings
Prep and Cook Time: 20 minutes

Ingredients

- 1½ lbs salmon filet, cut into 4 pieces, skin and bones removed
- ½ Tbsp maple syrup
- 1 large cucumber, peeled, cut in half lengthwise, seeds scooped out, diced in ½ inch cubes
- 1 large ripe fresh tomato, seeds, excess pulp removed, diced
- 1 medium ripe, but firm avocado, diced in ½ inch cubes
- 2 Tbsp chopped chives
- 1½ Tbsp chopped fresh dill
- 3 Tbsp fresh lime juice
- 1 Tbsp olive oil
- sea salt and black pepper to taste

Preparation

1. Mix together cucumber, tomato, avocado, chives, and dill in a bowl and set aside.
2. Whisk together 2 Tbsp lime juice, olive oil, sea salt and pepper in a separate bowl. Toss with cucumber mix when ready to serve.
3. Preheat a stainless steel skillet over medium high heat for 2 minutes.
4. Rub salmon with 1 Tbsp lime juice and season with sea salt and pepper.
5. Place in hot pan bottom side up. Cook for 2 minutes. While cooking, mix together maple syrup.
6. Turn salmon and spread maple syrup on top of fish. Continue to cook for another 2 minutes, depending on how thick salmon is. You want it pink on the inside. Season with pepper.
7. Divide cucumber mixture between 4 plates and serve with salmon.

Southwestern Snapper Sauté

4 servings
Prep and Cook Time: 25 minutes

This makes a satisfying one-dish meal as it is, or can be served with warm corn tortillas for a fresh, healthy and low-fat taco meal.

Ingredients

➢ 1 medium onion, cut in half and sliced medium thick
➢ 1-2 tsp minced jalapeno pepper, seeds removed, or to taste
➢ 1 Tbsp vegetable stock (broth)(pg 95)
➢ 2 cups diced zucchini (1/2 inch cubes)
➢ 1lb snapper filet cut into 1 inch pieces
➢ 15 oz fresh diced cherry tomatoes
➢ 3 Tbsp fresh lime juice
➢ 2 Tbsp chopped fresh cilantro
➢ 1 Tbsp chopped fresh oregano
➢ 1 ripe but firm medium avocado, diced into 1 inch pieces
➢ sea salt and black pepper to taste

Preparation

1. Heat 1 Tbsp broth in a 10-12 inch stainless steel skillet.
2. Sauté onion in broth over medium heat, stirring frequently for 5 minutes.
3. Add zucchini and jalapeno, and continue to sauté for another 2 minutes.
4. Add snapper and continue to sauté for another 2 minutes, stirring frequently.
5. Add rest of ingredients, except avocado, and cook for another 2 minutes. Add avocado, season with sea salt, pepper and serve.

Chapter Ten

SUPPLEMENTAL PRODUCTS LIST

ALKALINE FOODS SUPPLEMENTS

These products can be found at your local health foods store or online.
Website: http://www.alkalinefoodsllc.com

BLOOD TONIC

Blood Tonic is a special blend of herbs designed for internal cleansing, nourishment and support of the blood, liver and immune system. It helps keep the blood clean and free of impurities, and supplies it with vital iron, the "energy giver." It attracts oxygen and builds blood.

It is rich in natural occurring plant base iron, manganese, copper, zinc, sulfur, phosphorus, chromium, and contains easily absorbed calcium & magnesium which tones and relaxes the nervous system, relieving tension due to stress and the associated headaches. Natural occurring vitamins are A, B-1, B-6, B-12, C, E, and more.

MALE TONIC

Male Tonic is a special blend of herbs designed for internal cleansing. It provides naturally occurring zinc for nourishing support for the prostate gland it promotes testosterone and improves sexual dysfunction by correcting hormonal deficiency. Male Tonic may improve the urinary flow rate and may regulate shrinkage in the size of the prostate caused by benign prostatic hyperplasia (BPH). Consumption of Male Tonic can result in significant amelioration of symptoms, reduction in prostate size, and clearance of bladder neck urethral obstruction. Also helps with erectile dysfunction and impotency, depression, poor memory, and acts as an anti-inflammatory.

FEMALE FORMULA

Female Formula cleanses, nourishes, and balances the female endocrine system. It restores healthy menses and soothes irritation and congestion of the cervix, uterus and vagina. It is commonly used to relieve lower back pain and cramps caused by menstruation. Excellent for pre-menopausal and menopausal women to tone, balance, and strengthen female hormonal systems. It supports the reproductive system by strengthening the tissues of the womb, increasing lactation and easing nausea caused by morning sickness. It has a calming effect on the central nervous system, and helps in increasing libido, while decreasing fatigue. It may help insomnia related to hypertension and agitation.

VIRAL PLEX

Viral Plex is an antiviral, antivenin, cough suppressant, antibacterial, digestive stimulant, protease inhibitor (typically used for viral infections), and anti-inflammatory formula. It is effective in supporting our body's immune and circulatory systems and promoting healthy cholesterol levels. It includes a salt of elenolic acid, demonstrated to act strongly against many viruses, bacteria and parasitic protozoans. Among other effects, the compound was found to be potent against a variety of viruses associated with the common cold.

COLON REPAIR

Colon Repair is a special blend of herbs designed for internal and cellular cleansing, providing nourishing support to improve the muscle tone of the colon walls. It is excellent for clearing toxins from the digestive system and has a deeply purifying effect of the colon. It goes deep into the cells walls and releases the toxins at a much deeper level than your ordinary colon cleanses. It removes toxins up to and including the fat cells. In addition, it detoxifies the cells, blood, muscles and organs, it acts as a bowel cleanser and anti-inflammatory for Crohn's, colitis, diverticulitis, irritable bowel syndrome (IBS), and other bowel problems, stomach ulcers and ulcerative colitis and as an ulcer preventative/ stomach and bowel protector. It helps with muscle pains, strains and injuries, as well as preventing skin disease. Colon Repair also helps balance cholesterol and hypoglycemic actions, or lowering blood sugar.

ALKALINE FOODS GREEN FOOD PLUS

Green Food Plus is a special blend of alkaline greens nutritional foods containing a great variety of vitamins, minerals, important trace elements and chlorophyll, all of which possess powerful antioxidant properties. Green Food Plus infuses your body with easily absorbed phytonutrients and alkaline minerals that help to neutralize acids in the blood and tissues.

Green grasses and sea vegetables are some of the most alkalizing foods on the planet. Greens are very rich in chlorophyll, which is often called "the blood" of plants. The molecular structure of chlorophyll is the same as human blood with the exception of the center atom, which is magnesium rather than iron. Your body has the ability to convert the center atom of chlorophyll with iron to form and build the blood. Chlorophyll helps the blood cells deliver oxygen throughout the body.

Green food plus can be mixed with water or juices and in shakes, sprinkled on food, or used as an ingredient while cooking.

SEA MOSS MIX

Sea moss Mix offers 92 of the 102 minerals of which the body is made. It is helpful for the bones, thyroid and glands, bad breath, pulmonary and respiration illnesses, coughs, and dysentery. It also dissolves fat, acts as a natural diuretic, calms the appetite, aids digestion, prevents ulcers, and promotes regular bowels. It includes calcium, vitamins A & B complex, iron, fluoride, potassium, polysaccharides, iodine, bromine, mucilage, carrageenans, beta carotene and protein. Drink freely daily.

STAY ALKALINE!

LaVergne, TN USA
15 March 2011
220228LV00006B/209/P